THE NEW
SCROOGE
INVESTING

OTHER BOOKS BY MARK SKOUSEN

ACADEMIC

Playing the Price Controls Game
The Structure of Production
Economics on Trial
Dissent on Keynes (editor)
The Investor's Bible: Mark Skousen's Principles of Investment
Puzzles and Paradoxes in Economics (coauthored with Kenna C.
  Taylor)
Economic Logic
The Making of Modern Economics

FINANCIAL

The Insider's Banking & Credit Almanac
High Finance on a Low Budget (coauthored with Jo Ann Skousen)
The Complete Guide to Financial Privacy
Tax Free
Scrooge Investing
Mark Skousen's 30-Day Plan for Financial Independence

THE NEW SCROOGE INVESTING

The Bargain Hunter's Guide to Thrifty Investments, Super Discounts, Special Privileges, and Other Money-Saving Tips

Mark Skousen

McGraw-Hill

New York   San Francisco   Washington, D.C.   Auckland   Bogotá
Caracas   Lisbon   London   Madrid   Mexico City   Milan
Montreal   New Delhi   San Juan   Singapore
Sydney   Tokyo   Toronto

Library of Congress Cataloging-in-Publication Data

Skousen, Mark.
    The new scrooge investing : the bargain hunter's guide to thrifty investments,
super discounts, special privileges, and other money-saving tips / by Mark Skousen.
      p. cm.
    Includes index.
    ISBN 0-07-135500-6
    1. Investments. 2. Finance, Personal. 3. Saving and investment. I. Title.
HG4521.S614 2000
332.024—dc21

                                       99-054988

McGraw-Hill

A Division of The McGraw·Hill Companies

1 2 3 4 5 6 7 8 9 0 DOC/DOC   0 9 8 7 6 5 4 3 2 1 0

ISBN 0-07-135500-6

*The sponsoring editor for this book was Stephen Isaacs, the editing supervisor was
Janice Race, and the production supervisor was Elizabeth J. Strange. It was set in
Times New Roman.*

Printed and bound by R. R. Donnelley & Sons Company.

McGraw-Hill books are available at special quantity discounts to use as premiums
and sales promotions, or for use in corporate training programs. For more information, please write to the Director of Special Sales, Professional Publishing, McGraw-
Hill, Two Penn Plaza, New York, NY 10121-2298. Or contact your local bookstore.

This publication is designed to provide accurate and authoritative information in
regard to the subject matter covered. It is sold with the understanding that neither the
author nor the publisher is engaged in rendering legal, accounting, or other professional service. If legal advice or other expert assistance is required, the services of a
competent professional person should be sought.
—*From a Declaration of Principles jointly adopted by a Committee of the American
Bar Association and a Committee of Publishers.*

 This book is printed on recycled, acid-free paper containing a minimum of
50% recycled, de-inked fiber.

To Gary North, my favorite tightwad

Contents

Preface to the Third Edition   *ix*
Acknowledgments   *xiii*
Introduction: The Scrooge Philosophy
  of Investing   *1*

1. How to Find a Bargain Investment   7

**PART 1: THE SCROOGE
        STOCK INVESTOR**
2. Bargain Hunting for the Stock Buyer   17
3. Penny-Pinching on Penny Stocks   29
4. Which Discount Broker Is Best for You?   35
5. Saving Money on Mutual Funds   45
6. The Bargain Hunter's Guide to Higher
   Income and Capital Gains   63
7. Cutting the Cost of Holding Cash   79

**PART 2: THE ONLINE
        SCROOGE INVESTOR**
8. Scrooge Investing on the Internet   91
9. The Cheapskate's Guide to Unlimited Free
   Investment Information (Especially
   on the Internet)   101

**PART 3: THE NONTRADITIONAL
        SCROOGE INVESTOR**
10. Cutting Your Fees on Options and Futures   121

11. Saving Money on Precious Metals
    and Bargain Hunting for Mining Stocks   129
12. Saving Money When You Buy and Sell
    Real Estate   141
13. Saving a Bundle on Rare Coins,
    Collectibles, and Antiques   151
14. Slashing Fees on Offshore Investments
    and Foreign Currencies   165

PART 4: MORE SCROOGE INVESTING
15. Low-Cost Methods of Borrowing Money   183
16. Cutting Your Biggest Investment
    Costs—Taxes!   193
17. More Discounts and Benefits for Scrooge
    Investors   209
18. Conclusion: The Philosophy of the Scrooge
    Investor in the New Millennium   223

Index   *229*

Preface to the Third Edition

Most of the great investors are misers.

—*Warren Buffett*

E ureka!" That's what Scrooge McDuck would say to the incredible response to the first two editions of *Scrooge Investing*. Why has *Scrooge Investing* struck a chord among investors?

Two reasons. First, by spending less, you put your money in your pocket. There's no fun in overpaying, paying too much to brokers to buy overvalued stocks, real estate, or airline tickets. And it happens all too often.

Second, one of the supreme joys in life is finding a bargain. There's no better conversation topic at a cocktail party than telling everyone about the cheap stock you tripled your money on, the used car you bought at half the bluebook value, or the foreclosure you picked up and sold for a $25,000 profit in one month—all using online brokers!

I love being a Scrooge Investor. (And by Scrooge Investor, I mean the fun-loving Disney character Uncle Scrooge McDuck, not the misanthropic Dickens character Ebenezer Scrooge!) How can I forget the day that . . .

. . . One of my students bought America Online at $7 and held on as it rose to over $200 a share (split adjusted).

. . . I saved $10,000 buying a first edition of Adam Smith's 1776 classic *Wealth of Nations* by buying through my art discount dealer.

. . . The Republicans won control of Capitol Hill in November 1994, and I told my income-seeking subscribers to buy an income fund yielding 9.1 percent tax-free (the symbol was VOT!), only to see the fund jump 24 percent in three months. (As I told my subscribers, "Vote for VOT!")

. . . One of my readers picked up a Parker Aztec gold pen for only $55 at a garage sale and sold it to a specialty dealer for $15,000!

. . . My friend and I got into an Oakland Athletics sold-out baseball game for $5 and sat in the tenth row.

. . . My wife and I flew to Hong Kong and were bumped up to business class for free (a savings of over $5000).

Being a Scrooge Investor (and consumer) is infectious. Everyone loves a bargain and hates overpaying. Everyone wants to be a bargain hunter and the object of admiration. This book, chock-full of practical advice, will show you the way.

When I began updating this edition of *Scrooge Investing,* I had no idea how much things had changed in a mere four years since the previous edition. So we named this edition appropriately *The New Scrooge Investing.* It's at least 50 percent new!

The biggest change is the Internet, which has transformed—even revolutionized—the modus operandi of the Scrooge Investor. The Internet has provided a new, exciting way to shop, invest, sell, discover, and communicate. And the bargains have never been more tempting.

Because of the Internet and Web sites, I revamped entirely Chapter 2 on bargain hunting for stock market investors, Chapter 4 on discount brokers, Chapter 7 on holding cash, Chapter 9 on the cheapskate's guide to investment information, and Chapter 13 on collectibles and auctions. Plus, I added an entirely new Chapter 8, Scrooge Investing on the Internet. Don't miss it.

You'll notice in this edition that I've beefed up all the chapters related to the stock market. The bull market on Wall Street has attracted a whole new breed of investors and speculators, including day traders. Over half the book is now devoted to stock market profits and how to avoid the pitfalls. The Scrooge Investor must be at all times alert to avoiding overpriced stocks as well as to picking bargains.

As you will quickly see, the Scrooge investment philosophy applies to all markets and all conditions, whether buying or selling, investing or consuming. There are chapters on stocks, bonds, mutual funds, real estate, art and collectibles, gold and silver, foreign currencies, penny stocks, borrowing money—you name it. The purpose of this guidebook is to introduce the philosophy of the Scrooge Investor and to offer numerous up-to-date examples.

Most important, *time* is of the essence for today's fast-paced investors. One of the big benefits of *The New Scrooge Investing* is that it does the homework for you, so you don't have to waste a lot of time finding the cheapest brokers, art dealers, term insurance, mutual fund, or foreign bank account. We've done the work for you.

In writing these various editions of *Scrooge Investing,* I've been struck many times by two special areas. First, there's the use of closed-end funds as a way to find incredible bargains in the stock market, a way to buy undervalued stocks and bonds at a discount (see especially Chapters 1, 5, 6, and 14). Second is the unbelievable savings my readers have gained through my discount art dealer, Fine Arts Ltd., when they buy art and collectibles, probably the most overpriced investments in the world. It's truly amazing how many letters and e-mails I've received over the years from subscribers who have saved thousands of dollars on paintings, prints, rare books, sculptures, and collectibles. See Chapter 13 for more details on that.

We have attempted to update all the information from previous editions as much as possible, but information changes rapidly in the twenty-first century. Be sure to call the sources and references before acting on any advice. Always be up-to-date before acting. Also, check the most recent issue of my newsletter, *Forecasts & Strategies,* for current advice and recommendations, or check the Web site, www.forecasts-strategies.com. See also my new Web site, www.scroogeinvesting.com, which updates all the information in this book on a regular basis.

Yours for freedom and prosperity,

Mark Skousen
Editor, *Forecasts & Strategies*

Acknowledgments

Many people have helped in preparing this new edition. I would not go so far as to say that we spared no expense to get you this information. That would not fit our Scrooge philosophy. But we did pay what was necessary to obtain the best and most current information for you.

First and foremost, I want to thank Michael Ketcher, a freelance writer in St. Louis, for doing much of the spade work, checking details, making phone calls, and following up on leads. He spent literally hundreds of hours updating this new third edition. Without Mike's careful research, this edition would never have seen the light of day. I hesitate to call his freelance work entirely *free,* but it was quite a bargain. He almost—almost!—deserves to be coauthor.

Mike is an author, editor, and lecturer in his own right and knows how to dig for facts and the best expertise on any particular subject. Right now, he is editor of an alluring newsletter called *The Financial Privacy Report,* which I highly recommend (P.O. Box 1277, Burnsville, MN 55337; 612-895-8757; fax 612-882-4962; $144 a year/12 issues).

I would also like to thank the following for their help: Larry Abraham, Gary Alexander, Richard Band, Bert Blumert, Harry Browne, Charles Carlson, Doug Casey, Michael Checkan, Charlie Cox, Adrian Day, Bert Dohmen, Bill Donoghue, Doug Fabian, Alex Green, Greg Horne,

Vern Jacobs, Bob Kephart, Michael Kuschmann, Dave Phillips, Rick Rule, John Schaub, Gary Scott, Van Simmons, Jo Ann Skousen, Tim Skousen, Kevin Smith, John Templeton, Paul Terhorst, Tommy Thompson, Martin Truax, Andrew Westhem, Jack White, Richard Young, and Peter Zipper.

Finally, I'd like to extend my appreciation to editor Stephen Isaacs at McGraw-Hill as well as to former editor Roger Marsh for their enthusiastic support for a third edition of *Scrooge Investing*.

THE SCROOGE PHILOSOPHY OF INVESTING

Save your money, nephew! Pennies saved today
are dollars in your pocket tomorrow!

—*Uncle Scrooge McDuck*

THE SCROOGE PHILOSOPHY OF INVESTING reminds me of the shrewd investor's favorite fictional character: Uncle Scrooge McDuck.

One of my prized possessions in my trophy case at home is a limited-edition artwork entitled *Uncle Scrooge McDuck: His Life and Times,* written by his creator, Carl Barks. It is a beautiful four-color reproduction of Uncle Scrooge's most popular tales between 1952 and 1967.

As part of the purchase, I received a limited-edition color print of *Wanderers of Wonderlands,* a classic drawing of Uncle Scrooge along with Donald Duck and Huey, Dewey, and Louie examining a newfound treasure of gems. The print is autographed by Barks.*

This collector's edition brings back a lot of memories. In the 1950s, I grew up on Uncle Scrooge comic books. As a child, I was fascinated by Uncle Scrooge and his adventures with his nephews, his ingenuity in discovering new sources of boundless wealth, and his ability to thwart the schemes of the thieving Beagle Boys.

I have tried to pass along these boyhood memories to my five children. When I first received the book, I broke the plastic seal around it and read each story aloud to five eager listeners. I realize that it's a no-no actually to use a collectible. You're supposed to preserve its pristine condition to maintain its highest resale value. (I guess I should have hidden it away in a dark safe-deposit box to avoid all human touch.) I suppose it lost some of its collector's value, but the lessons and joy my children have gained from it far outweigh any monetary reward.

After reading the stories, I carefully returned the book to the trophy case and warned the children not to take it down on their own. Apparently, the temptation was too strong, and I often found the book outside the trophy case. Stern warnings didn't seem to help. They liked the stories too much and just couldn't resist.

THE APPEAL OF UNCLE SCROOGE
Barks introduced Uncle Scrooge in a Donald Duck comic book in the late 1940s. Uncle Scrooge soon became Walt Disney's top-selling comic book in the 1950s, ahead of Donald Duck and Mickey Mouse. What makes this irascible character so appealing to Americans? He is based on another popular fictional miser, Ebenezer Scrooge, Charles Dickens's famous character in *A Christmas Carol*.

* Now in his nineties, Barks is living in California, no longer an active artist. For more information about his life and to see many of his famous color drawings, go to www.yahoo.com and search the name Carl Barks.

Despite his extreme stinginess and fanaticism, there is something universal in Uncle Scrooge's character that can appeal to everyone. His zeal for material wealth gave him many virtues: hard work, individualism, ingenuity, integrity, determination, boldness, adventurousness, and a sense of humor. Yes, he is a skinflint who is not responsive to charitable causes, but he is always willing to get others involved in pursuing a dream.

Above all, Uncle Scrooge is not deceptive or dishonest as so many tycoons are currently portrayed on television and in the movies. Scrooge earned every penny of his hoard honestly. (The real thieves are the Beagle Boys.) In the first all-Scrooge comic in 1952, Scrooge described how he made his fortune as a gold digger. As Barks explained, "I never thought of Scrooge as I would think of some of the millionaires we have around today, who made their money by exploiting other people to a certain extent. I purposely tried to make it look as if Uncle Scrooge made most of his money back in the days when you could go out in the hills and find riches."

Scrooge not only made a fortune, he kept it. Unlike many instant millionaires, who tend to lose it as fast as they make it, Scrooge worked hard to keep every dime. "I froze my fingers to the bone, digging nuggets out of the creeks! And I brought a fortune out, instead of spending it in the honky-tonks!"

Uncle Scrooge has also been accused of being a hoarder. You probably remember the pictures of Scrooge diving into his money bin of gold and silver coins nearly 100 feet deep. But that's just for show. Scrooge called it his petty cash vault. What you don't see is his real fortune—the oil wells, railroads, gold mines, farms, factories, steamships, theaters, department stores, and radio stations he owns.

"I've invested in practically every business there is," he told Donald. Uncle Scrooge is the world's biggest investor, with bank accounts, stocks and bonds, and other liquid sources of wealth. A good investor puts his money to work! As he tells his nephews, "Saving money is the first important step to wealth . . . but I hope you realize I didn't get to be the world's richest duck just by salting my money away!"

HOW TO USE THE SCROOGE PHILOSOPHY TO MAKE MONEY

Like most Disney cartoons and comic books, Uncle Scrooge was not written solely for children's entertainment. He has many lessons for adults. The Scrooge philosophy is threefold:

- Look for bargain opportunities to make money.

- Always be cost-conscious; make the most of every penny you spend.

- Always do your homework; go out and check the facts yourself.

There's a little bit of Scrooge in all of us. You may not be a miser or self-centered, but you want to keep as much of your wealth as possible. The Scrooge philosophy is simple: The less you have to pay others, the more you keep for yourself. That is the essential theme behind this book.

In the investment world, saving money on commissions, fees, and other costs can make a big difference in what you keep. My findings demonstrate that by shopping around and selecting the right investment, broker, or banker, you can put thousands of dollars more in your pocket each year! In *Scrooge Investing,* I've broken down each investment area— stocks, bonds, gold, cash, collectibles, and foreign investments, among other,—to show how you can save thousands of dollars in each category.

You do not have to read each chapter in order. Feel free to go to any investment area you are interested in, and you'll see how much you can save.

The world's most successful business people and investors have always been bargain hunters. They avoid paying too much, whether for a business, a stock, or a collectible. People like John D. Rockefeller, J. Paul Getty, and Warren Buffett are always cost-conscious. Why? Because if costs get out of hand, a thriving business can quickly become unprofitable. Economists have shown time and time again that whether a business or investment is profitable depends on the margin. Those who are always on the lookout to eliminate unnecessary costs are the ones who survive recessions and outperform their competitors.

Even millionaires can go bankrupt if they disregard their costs and spend money foolishly. "A small leak can sink a great ship," Benjamin Franklin said.

It's not how much you make; it's how much you keep that matters. If you watch your costs closely, you'll be ahead of the crowd.

DON'T BE PENNY-WISE AND POUND-FOOLISH

This is not to say that you should be penny-wise and pound-foolish. There's nothing wrong with paying more for something as long as you get value for what you pay. A full-service broker may offer valuable information that a discount or an online broker doesn't have. A stock or mutual fund that you have to pay a broker to buy may far outperform a no-load mutual fund. Expertise has its price. Just make sure you don't pay for it too dearly. Follow Uncle Scrooge's dictum: Always use the cheapest way to get what you want! Pay what is necessary and no more!

Uncle Scrooge is never a passive investor, and neither should you be. Always be active and up-to-date and you will succeed like never before in your business and your portfolio. Uncle Scrooge never relies on magic or mechanistic formulas to get rich, and neither should you. There is no substitute for hard work. And there's nothing like the thrill of victory in the investment markets . . . or the agony of defeat!

Here's hoping this special book will help you along the way.

Happy bargain hunting, investment misers!

1

HOW TO FIND A BARGAIN INVESTMENT

The veteran investor objectively looks for bargains in growth stocks, which he buys and holds for the long bull rise and takes dips and slumps in stride.

—*J. Paul Getty*

L ET ME REPEAT the three principles of Scrooge Investing:

- Look for bargain opportunities to make money.

- Always be cost-conscious.

- Always do your homework.

This chapter focuses on improving your ability to discover bargains in the marketplace, based on my 25 years' experience in the investment business. First, you need to decide what kind of investor you are. Essentially, there are two kinds of investors, conservative and speculative. Conservative investors are not interested in trading the market, so they avoid short-term trading in stocks, options, or futures. They are more interested in finding an investment they can live with for a long time. They want to buy and hold.

Speculative investors, on the other hand, enjoy trading in and out of markets frequently. Options and futures are ideal vehicles for the speculator. They may also trade a hot stock or even sell a stock short for quick profits. There are lessons to be learned for both types of bargain hunter.

BARGAIN HUNTING FOR THE CONSERVATIVE INVESTOR
Let's consider the techniques useful to conservative investors in finding bargains.

Temporary versus Permanent Bargains
First, be on the lookout for investments that are *temporarily* undervalued, not permanently undervalued. There's a big difference. A stock that is permanently undervalued is in a major bear market with little or no likelihood of a turn-around. The company may be suffering from negative earnings with little possibility of consistent positive earnings in the future. It may be headed for bankruptcy. Pan Am is a classic example. In the late 1980s, investors who purchased Pan Am at $2 a share may have thought they were getting a bargain, but they ended up seeing it fall to zero and lost all their investment. Permanently undervalued securities may rally from time to time, but these are nothing more than bear-market rallies, not the start of a genuine recovery.

Conservative investors must look for bargain stocks that have a decent chance of turning around. IBM and GM in early 1990s are classic examples. Both these blue-chip companies struggled in the early 1990s, while the rest of the market headed higher. Both companies reorganized and hired new CEOs in an effort to rebuild. Since then, the price of GM has doubled and that of IBM has quadrupled.

Today, many analysts think companies such as Compaq Computers and Nissan Motors are turnaround stories. Only time will tell whether they are temporarily or permanently undervalued.

Bargains in Bear Markets

Another source of bargains is to buy the stock of solid companies during a widespread bear market or a crash. Examples include 1962, 1973, 1982, 1987, and 1994. If you purchased stocks in healthy companies during these periods, you would have seen substantial profits a year or two later. Of course, profits were realized because the economy was essentially sound and the government didn't screw things up. If they had, these stocks would have stayed in limbo.

Changes in Government Policy

Conservative investors should be alert to changes in government policy and their effect on stocks, bonds, real estate, gold, and other investments. If the government raises taxes on business and individuals, it could slow economic growth and eventually cause a slump in the economy and the stock market. If the Federal Reserve imposes a tight-money, high-interest-rate policy, the result could be a recession and a slump in the prices of stocks and other assets. On the other hand, cutting taxes and easing monetary policy could stimulate the economy and boost stock prices and real estate.

Be on the lookout for a change in policy. It could mean a bargain in the making.

Emerging Markets Offer Opportunities

This principle applies around the world. If a nation changes its policy in favor of free markets, foreign capital, lower taxes, less inflation, privatization, denationalization, and open borders, its stock market may skyrocket in value. Assuming these changes are permanent, investors who get in early will be generously rewarded. Recent examples include emerging markets such as Mexico, Chile, Argentina, India, Turkey, and China. Conversely, when nations adopt antigrowth measures, such as raising taxes, tightening the money supply, and imposing socialism, investors would be wise to get out before it's too late.

The summer of 1997 was a classic example of overvalued stocks in Asia. Countries like Thailand, Indonesia, Korea, the Philippines, and Hong Kong had tied their currencies to the U.S. dollar while engaging in a government-induced credit boom. This credit boom created a massive price inflation in Asian stocks, real estate, and incomes. When the dollar rose 30 percent during the second half of the 1990s, Asian exports were regarded as too expensive, and speculators and institutional investors withdrew their funds from the area, causing a crash and a depression.

Of course, a crash always offers opportunities to buy bargains. Indeed, the stock markets in Korea, Singapore, and other parts of Southeast Asia had bounced back remarkably by 1999. These are the kinds of opportunities speculators are looking for.

Bargains in Mining Stocks

One of the most cyclical areas of the stock market is in gold shares and mining stocks in general. During a bull market in gold and commodities, which usually ends in a frenzied buying spree, it is not uncommon to see investors make 1000 percent on their investments in exploratory mining companies (often called penny stocks). The most recent bull market in gold stocks was 1996. You want to take your profits quickly, though, since bear markets in mining stocks can be treacherous and lengthy. Many junior gold stocks fell 90 percent from their lofty levels of 1996. After this bloodbath, bargains are starting to develop again in this area.

UNDERVALUED PLAYS IN NEW ISSUES
AND CLOSED-END FUNDS

Watch for bargains in new issues and closed-end mutual funds. I discuss these ideas later in the book. Studies show that you should generally wait before buying new issues, although there are always exceptions to this rule (such as America Online and other Internet stocks in the late 1990s). Usually, the best time to buy is after two years, when the newness of the public company has worn off and the stock is fairly valued. According to a study by *Forbes,* most new issues rise above their offering price at first, then come back down after two years and then usually sell for less than their offering price! If you buy then and the company is making strong earnings, you are bound to do well.

By the same token, don't buy equity closed-end funds when they first come out. They usually sell at a discount after the new issue date. The best bargains come when investors become disenchanted after a few months or years and dump the fund, so it sells substantially below its net asset value (NAV). Check *Barron's* or the Monday edition of *The Wall Street Journal* for a list of all closed-end funds. Consider buying closed-end funds selling at 20 percent or more below their NAVs. They are likely to recover at some point. Likewise, avoid buying closed-end funds that sell substantially above their NAVs. These hot funds are likely to turn cold soon.

My subscribers and I have made considerable profits buying low-priced closed-end income funds from time to time. See Chapter 6 for details.

BE A CONTRARIAN

Ultimately, the key to bargain-hunting is to be a contrarian investor. Being a contrarian is easier said than done. Everybody wants to be a contrarian. Obviously, everyone can't get out at the top or buy at the bottom, because prices are always determined by a marginal number of buyers and sellers. Only a small percentage of sellers can get out at the top, and only a small number of buyers can get in at the bottom. Only a minority of investors can beat the market. Many academic studies have proven this truism.

The best approach to picking up a bargain is to wait until a market has turned around and then, if the economic fundamentals are favorable, to buy. You won't get in at the exact bottom, but you will get aboard early in the trend and should do quite well. However, this approach takes a great deal of patience. You sometimes have to wait years before a bargain turns up in a particular market.

Humphrey B. Neill, father of contrarian thinking, once said, "The public is right during the trend, but wrong at both ends." The only problem is knowing when the trend reverses itself. It may last longer than you expect. Sensing when a trend is changing is more an art than a science. It takes years of experience to recognize it.

ADVICE FOR SPECULATORS

Some of you, no doubt, are looking for quick profits. Often, the biggest profits are made at the basement level of markets. The first move up in an undervalued investment is usually the strongest and most profitable. Similarly, when stocks fall, the bear market is usually swift and dramatic. Bull markets stretch over long periods of time; bear markets usually are short-lived. As a speculator, you have to be nimble and your decisions well-timed. Timing is everything for the short-term trader.

Speculators should have a firm grasp of basic economics and fundamental analysis, even though they will probably rely mostly on technical factors to determine when to get in and out of markets.

George Soros, financial wizard of the billion-dollar Quantum Fund, uses both sound economics and technical trading methods to profit around the world. His most famous coup was making $1.5 billion in September 1992 (one month!) from the collapse of the European currency arrangement. He knew that the German mark was undervalued and the British pound and Italian lira were overvalued. It was only a matter of time before a realignment would take place. When the Berlin Wall came down in late 1989, Soros knew that in a few years, the whole European currency deal had to fall apart. He placed his bets in the summer of 1992, when German officials said they would not support the British pound forever, and when Britain and Sweden raised interest rates sharply, which he knew could not last.

Speculators must always be on the lookout for hot markets in individual stocks, country funds, and currencies. There is almost always a fundamental economic reason for these markets heating up or cooling down. Once the fundamentals take over in a market, the technical factors quickly confirm them and huge profits can be made.

A QUICK SUMMARY

Whether you are a conservative investor or an aggressive speculator, you can always find lots of bargains in the financial markets. Be sure to understand the fundamental economic reasons why an investment is undervalued or overvalued, and then take advantage of the moods of the market to determine when to get in or out.

Bonne chance!

PART 1

THE SCROOGE
STOCK INVESTOR

2

BARGAIN HUNTING FOR THE STOCK BUYER

I got rich because I always made my own lucky breaks.

—*Uncle Scrooge McDuck*

THE BARGAIN HUNTER AND THE CONTRARIAN INVESTOR are always on the lookout for a good deal on Wall Street, a cheap stock or mutual fund they can buy without paying much in commissions and bid-ask spreads. That's what this chapter is all about—cheap stocks, undervalued funds, new issues, and dividend reinvestment plans (DRIPs). DRIPs have been a great way to accumulate good companies without a broker, although, as you will see, DRIPs aren't the bargain they used to be.

$CROOGE INVESTING TIP #1

Buy Large-Cap Stocks With Low P/E Ratios

David Dreman, a money manager and *Forbes* columnist, has long recommended buying large-cap blue-chip stocks with low price/earnings ratios. Why? Because they are generally out of favor and will more likely move up more quickly than stocks with high P/E ratios. In his latest book, *Contrarian Investment Strategies: The Next Generation,* Dreman shows how stocks that sell cheaply in relation to their earnings are likely to beat the market.

Research by James P. O'Shaughnessy in his book, *What Works on Wall Street,* confirms Dreman's thesis. "High PE ratios are dangerous," warns O'Shaughnessy.

> Both large and all stocks with high PE ratios do substantially worse than the market. Companies with low PE ratios from the large stocks universe do much better than the universe. In both groups, stocks with low PE ratios do much better than stocks with high PE ratios.

$CROOGE INVESTING TIP #2

Buy Nasdaq Stocks!

Of course, neither Dreman nor O'Shaughnessy likes Nasdaq stocks, with their out-of-sight PE ratios. Yet Nasdaq stocks (mostly technology companies) have been superperformers in the 1990s and are likely to continue their superperformance in the new century. The New Economy is real! The best strategy is to buy Nasdaq stocks after a correction or crash. As J. Paul Getty says, "The seasoned investor buys his stocks when they are priced low, holds them for long-pull rise, and takes in-between dips and slumps in his stride."

Buying them individually, you are taking a gamble on Nasdaq stocks; many of them may not last due to intense competition. The best Scrooge Investor strategy is to buy the Nasdaq Index! Since 1995, the Nasdaq Index has doubled and then doubled again, going from 750 to over 3000. This trend is likely to continue. How to profit? Buy the Nasdaq 100 (AMEX: QQQ), or if you're more aggressive, buy the ProFund Ultra OTC Fund (symbol UOPIX, 800-776-3637), which aims to double the return of the Nasdaq 100 (by buying the Nasdaq 100 stocks on margin).

$CROOGE INVESTING TIP #3

IPOs Can Offer a Bonanza, but Beware!

With the booming stock market of the 1990s—and frenzied trading on the Internet—initial public offerings (IPOs) have become all the rage.

One of the advantages of buying a new issue is that the broker does not charge a commission. He or she is paid by the underwriter. However, new issues possess some hidden dangers. Remember, the firm is making the offering to make money, so it wants to get as much as it can for its shares.

Double-digit—and even triple-digit—gains in one day are not uncommon, especially in the wild and crazy world of Intenet IPOs. Barnesandnoble.com soared 27 percent in its first day of trading. The online brokerage firm DLJdirect jumped 50 percent. eToys nearly quadrupled in its first day of trading (but then dropped back to about one-third of its peak. One company, StarMedia Network, shot up 290 percent from its initial price of $15. In fact, one study shows that in early 1999 two-thirds of Internet IPOs doubled in their first day of trading.

According to a survey in *Forbes,* however, most new issues rise initially but two years later are selling below their offering price. If you're a buy-and-hold investor, like Warren Buffet, IPOs can be a gut-wrenching roller-coaster ride.

Consider what happened to Boston Chicken. It rose to $55 a few days after the stock went public in the fall of 1993. Then it quickly fell back to $40. By 1998, it had fallen to $4.50, and the company went into bankruptcy.

$CROOGE INVESTING TIP #4

Buy IPOs Through an Online Broker

Realize that you probably won't get in on the ground floor of any IPO. There are 11 large online brokers who receive allotments to sell a portion of IPOs that come on the market.

Some sell shares on a first-come, first-serve basis; others save them for their favorite customers. A lot of times it is the aggressive institutional traders who get first dibs, because they can buy large blocks of transactions. Shortly thereafter, they dump their stocks and small investors get caught holding the bag.

You also won't be getting your shares at the best price. Although there are no commissions, you will pay a markup, which can be up to 7–10 percent. Your discount stockbrokers, who may boast about $10 or $20 commission rates, really rake it in on IPO sales, making far more on the markup than they could ever dream of on the commissions from such sales.

$CROOGE INVESTING TIP #5

Get Lots of FREE or Low-Cost IPO Info on the Internet

The following Web sites will help you keep up-to-date on the latest IPOs:

- **Direct IPO** (www.directipo.com) will send you free e-mail updates about upcoming IPOs.

- **IPO Central** (www.ipocentral.com) has a guide for beginning IPO investors. You can also get profiles of companies and timetables of upcoming IPOs.

- **IPO.com** (www.ipo.com) contains current news and information about IPOs as well as offering documents from emerging companies.

- **IPO Data Systems** (www.ipodata.com) costs $15 a month, but it does give you considerable data about emerging companies, including prices, underwriters, attorneys, and auditors.

- **IPO Maven** (www.ipomaven.com) has daily, weekly, and monthly alerts on public offerings.

- **IPO Network** (www.ipo-network.com) monitors the performance of IPOs.

- **Wit Capital** (www.witcapital.com) is an Internet broker that specializes in IPOs. If you're a member, you can buy IPOs through the firm's Web site.

$CROOGE INVESTING TIP #6

Buy Closed-End Funds at Discounts of Up to 30 Percent!

If you really want out-of-favor sectors of the stock market, the best place to look is in *The Wall Street Journal* under Bargain Investments. What? you say. There's no such headline in the *Journal?* Look again. It's under the title, Closed-End Funds.

Closed-end funds are a great way to hunt for stock market bargains. These funds are investment companies that hold a portfolio of stocks, bonds, gold, or other assets and then issue a fixed number of shares. They trade on a stock exchange just like shares of IBM or General Motors. Hundreds of them are available, and they often trade at a discount to their net asset value or the value of the underlying stocks. *Barron's* and *The Wall Street Journal* list them each week.

The discount tells you a lot about the relative popularity of the sectors, such as computers, biotech, small caps, gold, or individual countries (so-called country funds).

I've seen discounts widen to as much as 50 percent, though most deeply undervalued funds sell for 25 to 30 percent of their NAV.

The Story of Convertible Holdings

Let me give you an example of how profitable buying deeply discounted closed-end funds can be. In 1991, Richard Band, a newsletter colleague, told me about Convertible Holdings Capital, which traded on the NYSE as symbol CNV. Convertible Holdings was known as a "dual purpose" fund, a little-understood vehicle that invests in a wide variety of convertible securities. The fund was split into two parts: the income sub-fund, which paid out all its dividends from convertible securities, and the capital subfund, which held the remaining assets. Over the years, the income subfund started selling at a premium, while the capital subfund began selling at a huge discount. When I first recommended the capital subfund, CNV, it had a net asset value of $8 a share but was selling for only $4, a whopping 50 percent discount!

Why would investors allow a fund to sell for only half the underlying value of its shares? First, because convertible securities are viewed as a strange hybrid and historically have not performed as well as growth stocks, nor do they provide the income other traditional income vehicles earn. Second, dual-purpose funds were at the time little-known vehicles that most investors had a hard time understanding. Third, the fund was divided up in a way that it would not pay any dividends or income. All income from the convertible securities would be paid out in its sister subfund, Convertible Capital Income, so the fund had to reflect its discounted value. And fourth, convertible securities are usually issued by firms less financially sound than blue-chip companies. For all these reasons, the original investors of CNV dumped the fund in the early 1990s as a "nonperformer."

However, when I looked at this fund in the early 1990s, I noticed a unique feature: In 1997, the closed-end fund was required by its bylaws to go open-ended or distribute all its shares to shareholders at its NAV. Either way, the discount must disappear.

Therefore, according to my calculations, if the stock market went nowhere in six years—which was highly unlikely—I was guaranteed to at least double my money! Now that's what I call a Scrooge Investor bargain. So I recommended it in my newsletter, *Forecasts & Strategies,* as well as the first and second editions of *Scrooge Investing,* and bought it myself.

Sure enough, over the years, two things happened. The fund increased in value, and the discount gradually disappeared. When the fund went open-ended in June 1997, it sold for $17 a share (including capital distributions), for a total return of 325 percent over six years. Not bad.

Other Examples

Let me give you a more recent example. Biotech stocks were hit hard in the mid-1990s, while computer and Internet stocks soared. In early 1999, at under $11 a share, the H&Q Life Science Fund (NYSE: HQL) was selling at a 27 percent discount from NAV. This was one of the highest discounts of any closed-end fund on the market.

I recommended it to my subscribers and the fund has since jumped to $15 a share, while the discount has fallen to 12 percent. It's no longer a superbargain, although biotech stocks are still hot as of this writing.

Another case is the Morgan Stanley Asia Pacific Fund (NYSE: APF). Asian stocks collapsed following the financial crisis of 1997, and MS Asia fell with everything else. In addition, the fund had a rights issue, which diluted it even further. By late 1998, MS Asia had drifted down to $5½ a share, selling at a 20 percent discount.

What has happened since then? It has made a major turnaround, along with Japan and the rest of Asia, in 1999. MS Asia has doubled in 1999 to over $10 a share, and the discount has fallen accordingly.

Not every closed-end fund that sells at a huge discount is guaranteed to recover. In fact, in the second edition of *Scrooge Investing,* I recommended Morgan Stanley Asia Pacific Fund at $10¼ because of its high discount. I also recommended the BGR Precious Metals Fund at $12¾ because of its 21 percent discount, and since then, the discount has remained the same and the price has fallen to $8. It too will have its day in the sun, but it may be a long time waiting.

Country Funds

Country funds are often a great way to "buy a whole nation" and benefit from a sudden bull market in a certain part of the world. Country funds in Brazil, Japan, Korea, and Mexico have been known to double or triple in value in one year. They can also lose half their value.

Warning: The level of discount from NAV is not always a reliable indicator of a country fund's future performance. Often, the discount may be more a reflection of the ease or difficulty you may have in investing directly in a country. For example, for years, the Korea Fund sold at a premium to NAV because that was the only way foreigners could invest in Korea. Now, however, Korea has eased up its restrictions, and the Korean funds (there are at least three) are all selling at a discount.

Check *Barron's* or the Monday edition of *The Wall Street Journal* for a complete list of country funds (under World Equity Funds). Typically, the country funds that do the best are the ones where government policy has suddenly changed in a positive way. On the other hand, the country funds with the worst performance are usually the ones with bad government policies. Very few country funds have shown the steady, rising performance of the United States.

Income Funds

Closed-end income funds are a great way to earn high income and capital gains—if you buy at the right time. See Chapter 14 for details.

One More Tip

Go to the Web site of the Closed-End Fund Association (www.closed-endfunds.com), perhaps the best Web site available on this obscure, but highly profitable, segment of the investment market.

$CROOGE INVESTING TIP #7

Avoid New Issues of Closed-End Equity Funds

You are almost always better off avoiding new issues of closed-end equity funds. They are generally offered at their full price, and perhaps even at a premium to their NAV, plus a full brokerage commission of 8.5 percent. Unfortunately, they usually fall to a discount within a few months of their initial offering, so wait for the drop before investing.

A recent study of the performance of IPOs of closed-end funds conducted by the Securities and Exchange Commission showed that after 24 weeks, U.S. closed-end equity funds had an average discount of 11.4 percent. Check out the pages of *Barron's* and *The Wall Street Journal.* Almost all closed-end equity funds sell at a discount, even in a roaring bull market. The lesson is clear: If you want to buy a closed-end fund, you're better off waiting until after the IPO is out.

$CROOGE INVESTING TIP #8

Eliminate Commissions With Dividend Reinvestment Plans—But Avoid the Pitfalls (There Are Many)
Dividend reinvestment plans (DRIPs) allow current shareholders to buy stock, usually without paying any commissions or transaction costs. Some 1200 companies currently offer DRIPs. Many of these firms (about 140) will allow you to buy these shares at a discount, sometimes up to 10 percent off the market price, although the typical discount is 2.5 to 5 percent. A few programs even allow you to borrow against the value of your shares as you can with a margin account at a brokerage firm.

Companies that give you such discounts include Bank of Boston, Citicorp, Citizens & Southern, Fleet/Norstar Financial Group, NMN Financial, J.P. Morgan, Security Pacific, Signet Banking, and Utilicorp United. Some plans allow you to make additional cash purchases directly from the company. However, purchases are usually restricted to a certain amount.

Unfortunately, DRIPs are not the great deal they once were. When you can buy shares of stock on the Internet for $5, you're not really saving much money. Meanwhile, many DRIPs have added charges—up to $5 a transaction and 12 cents a share! Such DRIPs are sometimes referred to as *direct purchase plans* (DPPs). Nevertheless, if you buy DRIPs that don't have fees, you can often buy fractional shares, in some cases investing as little as $10 to $25 a month. Such DRIPs are ideal for smaller investors.

You might also be charged a fee when you want to sell— a sales fee, a brokerage fee, or an account termination fee. Disney, for example, has the audacity to charge its plan members $10 plus 4 cents a share for the privilege of selling their shares. They add another $10 if you decide to end your participation in the plan.

In addition, with DRIPs there can be a lag time of nearly a week between the time your buy or sell order is placed and the time the trade is executed.

Another disadvantage: you can have fits trying to figure out your cost basis when you sell shares of a stock acquired through DRIPs. The only way to rectify this is to keep careful records. Some investors employ software programs, like Intuit's Quicken, to help them keep their records straight.

DRIP programs differ widely. With some, you must buy the first shares through a broker and then make subsequent purchases directly from the company. However, a growing number of the companies offering DRIPs allow you to buy your first shares directly. Currently, about 600 firms give you this option.

The terms for establishing and maintaining a DRIP account differ among firms. You'll have to check with the companies individually to see what their programs are. Seek out those DRIPs that allow you to invest for free, rather than those that charge a fee. Most flexible are those programs that allow you to buy a fixed dollar amount of the stock every month as opposed to a certain number of shares.

$CROOGE INVESTING TIP #9

Use National Discount Brokers' Free Dividend Reinvestment Program
With National Discount Brokers' free dividend reinvestment program, you can increase your stock positions without pay-

ing additional commissions or fees. It allows you to buy additional shares of an eligible stock by automatically reinvesting the cash dividends and capital gains that it pays. It also lets you reinvest fractional shares. You can choose to reinvest the cash dividends or capital gains of certain eligible positions or of your entire portfolio.

There's no charge to enroll in the program and you can change your selection at any time. The program is available with most stocks and closed-end funds listed on the NYSE, AMEX, and Nasdaq. For more information, contact: National Discount Brokers, 7 Hanover Square, 4th Floor, New York, NY 10004; 1-800-888-3999; www.ndb.com.

$CROOGE INVESTING TIP #10

Go to DRIP Central to Get the Latest Dope on DRIPS
You can find plenty of FREE information about DRIPs on the Internet.

One of the best Web sites for DRIP investors is DRIP Central (www.dripcentral.com). You'll find DRIP chat rooms, DRIP books and newsletters, and a DRIP database of over 800 companies that allow you to buy their stock without paying a commission.

Another worthwhile Web site for DRIP investors is Netstock Direct (www.netstockdirect.com). You can register for free and search the extensive DRIP database for companies that meet your criteria.

3

PENNY-PINCHING ON PENNY STOCKS

Patience in a market is worth pounds in a year.

—Ben Franklin

Y OU WOULDN'T THINK that a penny stock would be expensive, but investors routinely overpay, sometimes by as much as 40 percent, on penny and over-the-counter (OTC) stocks. Usually, they never know it. Just because a stock sells for less than $5 a share, which is now the standard definition of a penny stock, doesn't mean it's a bargain.

Some penny stocks, if bought wisely, can be tremendous bargains, and Uncle Scrooge is always interested in a bargain. Some of these small companies might have big profit potential. Just look at the Internet stocks!

Moreover, it's not unusual to find penny stocks trading at substantial discounts from their intrinsic (or cash) value and trading at ridiculously low price-earnings multiples of four or five.

The reason: These firms exist in an inefficient market that is largely overlooked by the Wall Street establishment.

The institutions and major brokerage firms ignore them, as do the national financial media—*Money* magazine, *Business Week, Forbes,* and *The Wall Street Journal.*

But the opportunities exist. You have much greater leverage with penny stocks than you do with most of the stocks trading on the New York Stock Exchange, the American Stock Exchange, or the upper tier of the over-the-counter, or Nasdaq, market. It is much easier to double your money in a stock selling for $0.50 to $1.00 than to double your money with IBM.

And just because a stock sells for a low price doesn't mean it's a small, insignificant company. Shares in the Hong Kong stock exchange regularly sell for less than $1 a share, yet they are often major blue-chip companies. (In general, many Asian stocks sell regularly for less than $1 a share. Asian investors like to think that small prices can turn into big values, and usually they're right.)

SCROOGE INVESTING TIP #11

Guard Against Excessive Markups

As we've seen with bonds, the commission isn't the only way your stockbroker makes money. In penny stocks and other OTC transactions, an aggressive broker can make a fortune by marking the stock up when you buy or marking it down when you sell. In fact, your broker may even try to trick you into thinking you're getting the transaction for free by telling you there is no commission. Indeed, your trade confirmation and client statement will bear this out. It won't reveal the huge profit the broker made on the spread (markup), the difference between the bid price and the ask price.

Here's how a stock is marked up: A $2.50 stock might be marked up by 0.75 of a point to $3.25. When sold, it might be marked down by 0.25 of a point to $2.25. It may not sound like much, but 1000 shares at 0.25 a point is $250.00. Multiply that by the thousands of shares sold and you can see how profitable it can be for some brokers. It's a good idea never to pay more than 20 percent higher than the market makers bid price. (The market maker is a brokerage firm that holds the stock in its own account.) If your broker is not a market maker, then he would go to the market maker to obtain the shares to sell to you.

$CROOGE INVESTING TIP #12

Instruct Your Broker to Act as Agent, Not Principal
If you ask the broker to act as your agent, he or she must give you the best available price at the time and fully disclose the commission on the order. Always ask your penny stock broker to act as agent rather than principal. If he or she refuses, go elsewhere or try to find out the spread and negotiate it down.

$CROOGE INVESTING TIP #13

Compare Price Quotes
It usually pays to compare price quotes from brokers. You could call several brokers, one right after the other, and buy from the one with the lowest quote, but this may not endear you to your broker. If you trade penny stocks, you might be better off opening an account with a brokerage firm that specializes in penny stocks. One such firm is Waterhouse Securities, Inc. (800-934-4410). In my survey of discount brokers, Waterhouse has the lowest fee for penny stocks. For penny stocks selling for under a dollar a share, Waterhouse charges $30 plus 3 percent of the principal. Many of my subscribers have had excellent relations with Waterhouse Securities.

$CROOGE INVESTING TIP #14

Don't Buy Right After a Newsletter Recommendation
Most penny stocks are thinly traded, with perhaps a few thousand shares changing hands daily. If a penny stock is recommended in a popular newsletter, the price can soar.

You're better off waiting two or three months until the buying frenzy has died down and the stock's price has settled back to more reasonable levels.

Don't buy a penny stock if it has already risen several hundred percentage points. Chances are you'll be getting in at or near the top of the market.

$CROOGE INVESTING TIP #15

Beware of Broker-Hyped Stocks
In general, if a broker calls you with a hot stock, you should hang up. No matter how exciting the deal sounds, no matter how glib the presentation, never invest solely on the sales pitch of a broker, particularly one you hardly know and have never dealt with.

$CROOGE INVESTING TIP #16

Ten Pointers on Penny-Stock Buying
Here is a penny-stock checklist:

1. Always scrutinize the annual report and any other literature you can obtain about a small firm, including brokerage company reports. Brokers sometimes exaggerate. Written information is more accountable to regulation and may put the investment in a more realistic light. Pay close attention to the footnotes and fine print.

2. Stay away from companies with excessive debt, that are in bankruptcy, or that are in need of raising capital soon.

3. Stay away from companies whose annual reports reveal too much of their assets under goodwill or that have negative working capital, poor earnings, or significant legal problems.

4. Stay away from penny stocks with high market capitalization. (The market capitalization is the market

value of a public company, determined by multiplying the number of issued shares by the trading price.)

5.   Look for liquidity. A stock should trade at least 50,000 shares a week. Penny stocks are *always* easy to buy, but if illiquid, they are hard to sell.

6.   Diversify your penny stock portfolio. You should invest in at least six companies.

7.   Ask brokers if they personally have a position in the stock they're recommending. Sometimes they do; sometimes they don't. If so, ask if they have sold or are planning to sell any and at what price they purchased the stock.

8.   Always take possession of penny stock certificates, unless they are foreign.

9.   In mining stocks, it's usually best to stick with firms that are in production or near it. Buying mining stocks in the earlier phases of growth exploration or the developmental stage is highly risky. You may be paying for a hole in the ground (often surrounded by liars)! It's difficult even for professional geologists and mining stock experts to assess the future prospects of these stocks. For more information on buying penny or junior mining stocks, see Chapter 11 on precious metals.

10.   Don't bet more than you can afford to lose. Penny stocks are highly speculative. Even if you've done your homework, you'll still probably lose your money. Take a chance on them only if that doesn't bother you.

4

WHICH DISCOUNT BROKER IS BEST FOR YOU?

Economy is in itself a great source of revenue.

—Seneca

DISCOUNT BROKERS ARE ESSENTIAL to the Scrooge Investor. You can save well over 90 percent by using the discounters over the full-service brokers. By carefully shopping among discounters, you can save even more money, paying virtually no commission in some cases.

Commission rates vary widely among discounters (see Table 4-1 on pages 37–39). Choosing the lowest-cost discounter is not always essential. Some of the higher-priced discounters may offer services that more than compensate for the higher commission rates. It is essential to choose a discounter that best meets your needs.

Even the highest-charging discounters, like Fidelity and Charles Schwab, are cheaper than the full-service (and full-priced) brokers. For example, if you were buying or selling 1000 shares of a $10 stock, Charles Schwab would charge

$110 and Fidelity $145. But Merrill Lynch would charge $264.60 for the same transaction.

Some offer toll-free quote lines, online trading through your personal computer, trading in no-load mutual funds, free or low-cost research, and other services. Others offer simply barebones, no-frills transactions. The companies listed in this chapter are among the country's leaders.

But don't just pick a company based on its commission rates. Call each company, get its literature, and read it carefully.

$CROOGE INVESTING TIP #17

Open an Account With One of These Six Major Discounters
One major problem with discount brokers is customer service. If you have a problem—*any* problem, ranging from a typographical error in your account statement to a botched transaction—you will need to get help.

Sometimes getting through to the right person is difficult. You may be put on hold interminably, listening to elevator music. You may not have your calls returned. It's sometimes enormously frustrating trying to get a problem taken care of over the telephone with someone in an office hundreds of miles away. It's easy for them to ignore you. Sometimes, phone systems even crash.

That's why I recommend that you use at least one discount broker with a branch office within an easy drive of your home. That way, if you have a problem, you can march right into the office and insist that your problem be taken care of while you wait. If the phones are down, you can place a buy or sell order right there.

If you travel frequently or have a vacation home, these larger discount brokerage firms will probably have an office close to where you are. That, too, may come in handy, since system crashes can occur wherever you are.

There are several firms that have branch offices across the country, and you should consider having an account at one of these firms, if they have an office near where you live.

TABLE 4-1   Discount Broker Survey

Sample 1: 20,000 Shares @ $0.50 per Share ($10,000)		Sample 2: 5000 Shares @ $1.00 per Share ($5000)	
Brown & Co	$105.00	Brown & Co.	$12.00
Ameritrade	18.00	Ameritrade	18.00
DLJ Direct		E*Trade	24.95
E*Trade	124.00	National Discount Brokers	24.95
National Discount Brokers	224.95	Barry Murphy	75.00
Barry Murphy	225.00	DLJ Direct	100.00
Scottsdale	285.00	Olde	152.50
Vanguard	300.00	Quick & Reilly	180.00
Olde	315.00	Vanguard	195.00
Waterhouse	330.00	Fidelity	250.00
Quick & Reilly	337.00	Waterhouse	250.00
Charles Schwab	439.00	Scottsdale	280.00
Fidelity	500.00	Charles Schwab	289.00

Sample 3: 1000 Shares @ $5.00 per Share ($5000)		Sample 4: 100 Shares @ $10.00 per Share ($1000)	
Brown & Co.	$12.00	Brown & Co.	$12.00
Ameritrade	18.00	Ameritrade	18.00
DLJ Direct	20.00	DLJ Direct	20.00
E*Trade	24.95	E*Trade	24.95
National Discount Brokers	24.95	National Discount Brokers	24.95
Olde	52.50	Barry Murphy	28.50
Barry Murphy	60.00	Scottsdale	35.00
Quick & Reilly	60.00	Waterhouse	35.00
Waterhouse	60.67	Quick & Reilly	37.50
Scottsdale	70.00	Olde	40.00
Vanguard	75.00	Charles Schwab	47.00
Charles Schwab	89.00	Vanguard	48.00
Fidelity	165.00	Fidelity	59.00

TABLE 4-1   Discount Broker Survey (*Continued*)

Sample 5: 1000 Shares @ $10.00 per Share ($10,000)		Sample 6: 500 Shares @ $20.00 per Share ($10,000)	
Brown & Co.	$12.00	Brown & Co.	$12.00
Ameritrade	18.00	Ameritrade	18.00
DLJ Direct	20.00	DLJ Direct	20.00
E*Trade	24.95	E*Trade	24.95
National Discount Brokers	24.95	National Discount Brokers	24.95
Olde	40.00	Barry Murphy	47.50
Barry Murphy	60.00	Scottsdale	55.00
Scottsdale	70.00	Vanguard	60.00
Vanguard	75.00	Waterhouse	61.32
Waterhouse	75.50	Olde	80.00
Quick & Reilly	84.00	Quick & Reilly	84.00
Charles Schwab	110.00	Charles Schwab	110.00
Fidelity	145.00	Fidelity	155.00

Sample 7: 200 Shares @ $30.00 per Share ($6000)		Sample 8: 300 Shares @ $40.00 per Share ($12,000)	
Brown & Co.	$12.00	Brown & Co.	$12.00
Ameritrade	18.00	Ameritrade	18.00
DLJ Direct	20.00	DLJ Direct	20.00
E*Trade	24.95	E*Trade	24.95
National Discount Brokers	24.95	National Discount Brokers	24.95
Waterhouse	37.99	Scottsdale	45.00
Barry Murphy	38.00	Barry Murphy	47.50
Scottsdale	40.00	Vanguard	54.00
Vanguard	51.00	Waterhouse	63.07
Olde	60.00	Olde	80.00
Quick & Reilly	65.00	Quick & Reilly	89.00
Charles Schwab	95.60	Charles Schwab	116.80
Fidelity	113.00	Fidelity	127.00

TABLE 4-1   Discount Broker Survey (*Continued*)

Sample 9: 500 Shares @ $50.00 per Share ($25,000)		Sample 10: 300 Shares @ $75.00 per Share ($22,500)	
Brown & Co.	$12.00	Brown & Co.	$12.00
Ameritrade	18.00	Ameritrade	18.00
DLJ Direct	20.00	DLJ Direct	20.00
E*Trade	24.95	E*Trade	24.95
National Discount Brokers	24.95	National Discount Brokers	24.95
Scottsdale	55.00	Scottsdale	45.00
Vanguard	60.00	Barry Murphy	47.50
Barry Murphy	62.50	Vanguard	54.00
Olde	100.00	Olde	80.00
Waterhouse	111.74	Quick & Reilly	115.25
Quick & Reilly	119.50	Fidelity	127.00
Charles Schwab	155.00	Charles Schwab	149.50
Fidelity	155.00	Waterhouse	207.00

Charles Schwab, Fidelity, Olde, Quick & Reilly, Scottsdale, and Waterhouse all have dozens of branch offices scattered across the United States. One of the lowest-cost brokers, Brown & Co., has 11 offices in major cities across the country.

$CROOGE INVESTING TIP #18

Look at Other Costs Besides Commissions
Many discount brokers entice you with low commission rates but nickel-and-dime you to death with other charges. These extra charges may not always be clearly spelled out in their advertising and other literature.

For example, a $10 to $15 charge if you want your stock certificate delivered to you is not uncommon among discount brokers. Some of the deep discount firms may charge you to wire funds to you, charge you for various services related to your IRA, charge you late payment fees, returned check fees, charge you for . . . well, you get the picture.

Also note that Table 4-1 lists commission rates only for market orders. These are orders that you place with your broker to buy or sell a specific number of shares at the best available price once the order is received in the marketplace. There is a higher fee for limit orders, in which you set a maximum buying price or a minimum selling price. With these, brokers can try to get a better price for you, but they cannot violate the limit price you set. Some firms will tack on an extra charge for limit orders, typically $5.

There are other oddball charges. Charles Schwab, for example, charges you $29 a year if you have less than $10,000 in your account, don't trade at least twice a year, or don't add money to your balance. Other companies may levy similar charges for "inactive" accounts.

Some of these charges won't affect you, and you don't have to worry about them. But the only way you'll find out is to read carefully the brochures, account agreements, and other literature they send you, including the fine print.

$CROOGE INVESTING TIP #19

Take Advantage of Deep Discount Brokers, Online Trading, and Touch-Tone Trading
Today, most discount firms offer you a choice between using a broker or trading online. If you don't have a computer, don't worry. At some firms you can get an extra discount by trading through your Touch-Tone telephone.

The commission rates in Table 4-1 are for broker-assisted trades. Generally, you'll save up to 25 percent for Touch-Tone telephone trades and 25 percent, 50 percent, or more by trading online. (Online trading is covered in Chapter 8.)

$CROOGE INVESTING TIP #20

Attention, Large Investors! Take Advantage of Superdiscount Brokers; You Can Even Trade Commission-FREE
Some discount brokers give a superdeal to larger investors (or average investors who want to grow large). These are the

superdiscounters. For example, Olde Discount Stockbrokers (800-USA-OLDE) offers commission-free trading on any listed common stock (must be listed on AMEX, Nasdaq, or NYSE; $5 or more per share; minimum 1000-share investment) as long as you have an account of $500,000 or more. Zero commissions! How do they do it? By charging fees and commissions on other products, such as bonds, options, and over-the-counter stocks.

Other firms offer other enticing deals. Brown & Co., for example, gives volume rebates of 10 percent whenever monthly commissions exceed $350.

Scottsdale offers a Supersaver Account in which you can make trades of up to 1000 shares for $50 per trade. To qualify, you must open the account with a minimum of $25,000 in securities or cash and must remain above $20,000 equity. You must also have sufficient buying power on deposit before you place a buy order and securities long (at least one week) in the account before they are sold.

Several other firms, including Charles Schwab, DLJ Direct, Fidelity, and National Discount Brokers, offer special perks to you if you have $100,000 or more in your account. These perks can include free research, a dedicated toll-free number, and better rates on cash balances or margin loans, depending on the firm and the amount of money in your account. If you're in this category, ask them for details.

I should also mention that the major full-service brokerage firms, such as Merrill Lynch and Salomon Smith Barney, are also offering "commission-free" trading if you sign up for their annualized billing system, which is 1.5 percent of the value of the account during the year. If you trade a lot, it could be a considerable savings.

$CROOGE INVESTING TIP #21

Choose a Discount Broker That Offers the Services You Need
Commission rates aren't the only factor in choosing a discount broker.

TABLE 4-2   How to Reach the Discount Brokers Surveyed in This Chapter

Ameritrade, 1003 N. Ameritrade Place, Bellevue, NE 68003; 1-800-454-9272; www.ameritrade.com.

Barry Murphy & Company, Inc., 77 Summer Street, Boston, MA 02110; 1-800-221-2111, 617-426-1770.

Brown & Co., One Beacon Street, Boston, MA 02108-3102; 1-800-822-2829; www.brownco.com.

DLJ Direct, One Pershing Plaza, Jersey City, NJ 07399; 1-800-825-5723; www.dljdirect.com.

E*Trade Securities, Inc., 2400 Geng Road, Palo Alto, CA 94303-3306; 1-800-ETRADE-1; www.etrade.com.

Fidelity Brokerage Services, Inc., 100 Summer Street, Boston MA 02110; 1-800-544-7272; www.fidelity.com.

National Discount Brokers, 7 Hanover Square, 4th Floor, New York, NY 10004-0533; 1-800-888-3999; www.ndb.com.

Olde, 751 Griswold Street, Detroit, MI; 1-800-682-6900, 313-961-6666; www.olde.com.

Quick & Reilly, 26 Broadway, New York, NY 10004-1899; 1-800-837-7220; www.qronline.com.

Charles Schwab & Co., The Schwab Building, 101 Montgomery Street, San Francisco, CA 94104; 1-800-435-4000; www.schwab.com.

Scottsdale Securities, Inc., 12855 Flushing Meadows, St. Louis, MO 63131; 1-800-906-SCOT, 314-965-1555; www.scottrade.com.

Vanguard Brokerage Services, P.O. Box 2600, Valley Forge, PA 19482-2600; 1-800-992-8327; www.vanguard.com.

Waterhouse Securities, Inc., 100 Wall Street, New York, NY 10005; 1-800-934-4410; www.waterhouse.com.

For example, do you trade mutual funds? If so, you'll want to choose a broker that offers the fund families you like. Do you need research? Then choose a broker that offers free or low-cost research reports.

Some firms offer frequent flyer miles. One of the best programs is TD Waterhouse's agreement with American Airlines to offer AAdvantage miles. You can get 10,000 miles when you bring $10,000 or more in new assets to a Waterhouse account; 1000 miles per year when you maintain a balance of $25,000 in your account throughout the year; and one mile for every $10 of your average monthly balance in the American AAdvantage Money Market Mileage Fund.

$CROOGE INVESTING TIP #22

Use Barry Murphy for Foreign Stocks

Many discount brokers don't handle foreign stocks. One that does is Barry Murphy & Co. Its normal rates on U.S. stocks are quite low. For foreign stocks, Murphy adds a flat $75 charge to normal commissions. Rates for American Depositary Receipts (ADRs) are the same as rates for other U.S. stocks.

ADRs are receipts for foreign corporations held in the vault in the foreign branch of a U.S. bank. Many large foreign corporations sell their stock in the United States in the form of ADRs. They trade over the counter (OTC) just like a U.S. OTC stock, but ADRs are not available for all foreign stocks. When ADRs are not available for a particular foreign stock, trade directly through Barry Murphy & Co.

5

SAVING MONEY ON MUTUAL FUNDS

There are few ways in which a man can be more innocently employed than in getting money.

—*Samuel Johnson*

MUTUAL FUNDS ARE, by definition, a low-cost way to get professional management and portfolio diversification. Even here, though, you must keep a watchful eye on commissions and other fees. These are listed at the beginning of each prospectus. Here's a rundown of what they are and how high they can go.

$CROOGE INVESTING TIP #23

Minimize the Hidden Fees and Commissions of Mutual Funds
Watch out for commissions, also called *loads*. These can range from zero to 5.75 percent. Competition has forced

high-load funds to reduce their loads from their historic highs of 8.5 percent to less than 5.75 percent in most cases. A 5.75 percent load, however, really amounts to a 6.1 percent load because the commission comes off the top. Loads reduce the size of the initial investment you make. For example, if you invest $1000 in a 5.75 percent-load fund, your initial account will start with $942.50. The $57.50 commission is 6.1 percent of $942.50.

Then there are management fees. Typically between 0.5 and 1 percent annually, they sometimes run 2 percent or higher on some funds. You can find out the *annual expense ratio* of a fund by referring to Morningstar, *Forbes,* or Schwab services at your local library or on the Internet.

Next, there are *12b-1 fees,* named after the SEC rule permitting them. These fees allow funds to pass their distribution and marketing costs on to investors, up to 2 percent, although most plans charge less than 0.5 percent. Like the management fee, it's paid to the fund's management annually out of the fund assets. Sometimes funds with 12b-1 fees are touted as no-loads, so it pays to read the prospectus.

To confuse matters further, some funds have *inactive 12b-1 plans.* They have installed the 12b-1 plan in case they want to impose it in the future, but they haven't implemented it and it doesn't cost you anything. Again, a careful reading of the prospectus will help, as will the figures quoted annually in Morningstar, *Forbes,* and other publications.

Redemption fees are sometimes charged to deter active trading. Typically 1 to 2 percent, they are often rescinded after you've held the fund for six months to a year. Schwab and other discount brokerage firms impose redemption fees on short-term tradings (usually 3–6 months).

Back-end loads or *contingent deferred sales charges,* often imposed by large brokerage firms on their "no-load" funds, can be especially costly. They are charged when you leave the fund. You might pay as much as 5 percent if you redeem your shares in the first year; the charge is decreased by 1 percentage point a year for the next five years.

$CROOGE INVESTING TIP #24

Choose No-Load and Low-Load Funds

I prefer pure (100 percent) no-load funds, although I occasionally recommend low-load funds, up to about 3 percent. I rarely recommend higher-commission funds.

Brokers often argue that a higher-commission fund is worth the extra money because the better performance will make up for the higher load in time. That's absolute nonsense. There's no logical reason why a sales charge paid to a broker would result in improved performance of the fund. The broker has nothing to do with how the fund performs.

In fact, the opposite is true. Sheldon Jacobs, author of *The Handbook for No-Load Fund Investors,* points out that "in 1998 the average no-load equity funds gained 12.7 percent compared to 8 percent for all equity funds as tracked by the *Lipper Mutual Fund Performance Analysis.*"

Jacobs' annual handbook is the most comprehensive source of information available for no-load fund investors, covering 2571 no-load and low-load funds. It costs $45, so check for it in your local library. To order or get a free sample of his newsletter, *The No-Load Fund Investor,* contact P.O. Box 318, Irvington-on-Hudson, NY 10533; 800-252-2042 or 914-693-7420.

Another drawback to load funds is that they almost force you to be a long-term investor. If you invest in a load fund and then change your mind, it can be quite costly. If you paid 5.75 percent to get into a load fund, you're immediately in arrears by 6.1 percent.

Forbes ranks mutual funds in a special issue every August/September, and its honor roll contains load and no-load funds. *Forbes* found no difference in performance between load and no-load funds.

$CROOGE INVESTING TIP #25

Buy the Funds With the Lowest Management Fee

In general, no-load funds have the lowest management and administrative fees. The average load fund has an expense ratio of 1.4 percent; the average no-load fund, 1.3 percent. High-fee funds can be expensive in more ways than one. A higher fee means less profits for you, and it can also mean more taxes because you are required to pay taxes not just on the dividends you earn but also on your share of the fund's gross income before management fees.

$CROOGE INVESTING TIP #26

Buy No-Load, Low-Fee Index Funds

Index funds invest in a portfolio of the securities that make up a popular index in the same proportional quantity as the index. Over time, they will mirror the performance of the index, minus a small administrative fee.

There are over 130 different index funds, the most popular being those that replicate the S&P 500. But there are funds that mirror other indexes, including foreign stocks, gold stocks, small-cap and mid-cap stocks, the Dow Jones 30 industrials, and others (see Table 5-1 for a sampling of what's available).

Saving Money on Index Funds

Index funds save you money in three ways.

1. They usually have lower management fees than most stock funds because, by comparison, they require much less expertise to manage. Some do impose fees (with expense ratios ranging from 0.5 percent to a little over 1 percent), which are payable to the fund rather than to the adviser or sales organization. Most are well under 1 percent. On the other hand, the average managed fund has an expense ratio of 1.44 percent, and some go as high as 3 percent.

2. *Index funds are tax-advantaged.* Because the managers of index funds only sell to meet redemptions by share-

TABLE 5-1 Low-Cost Index Funds

Fund	Duplicates Composition of	Annual Expense Ratio
American Century Equity Index (800-4-SAFETY)	S&P 500	0.49
Dreyfus S&P Index (800-645-6561)	S&P 500	0.50
Dreyfus S&P 400 MidCap Index	S&P 400	0.50
Federated MaxCap Fund (800-245-2423)	S&P 500	0.88
Federated MidCap Fund	S&P 400	0.89
Federated MiniCap Fund	Russell 2000	1.72
Fidelity Market Index (800-544-8888)	S&P 500	0.50
Gateway Index Plus (800-354-6339)	S&P 100, with options	1.15
Rushmore American Gas Index (800-621-7874)	109 natural gas companies	0.85
U.S. Global All American Fund (800-873-8637)	S&P 500	0.60
Vanguard Index T1 Bond Mk. (800-662-7447)	Salomon Bros Investment Grade	0.21
Vanguard Index Trust Extended Market	Wilshire 5000	0.23
Vanguard International Equity Index—Europe	Morgan Stanley EAFE Index	0.30
Vanguard International Equity Index—Pacific	Morgan Stanley Pacific Index	0.35
Vanguard Quantitative Index	S&P 500, using computer models	0.48
Vanguard Index Trust 500 Port.	S&P 500	0.23
Vanguard Small Cap Fund	Russell 2000	0.23

holders, there are few capital gains every year. Professor Jeremy Siegel of the Wharton School of Economics estimates that taxes and transaction costs (see #3) reduce returns by about 4.5 percent annually for most investors in actively managed funds. With index funds it's only 1.5 percent.

If a market crash were to occur, however, and index funds were hit with massive redemptions by shareholders, you could find yourself subject to a huge capital gains tax. The reason: Many index funds are sitting on stock that they bought cheaply. If they were forced to sell these low-priced stocks to meet redemptions, there would be some enormous capital gains. So far, despite several market crashes, we haven't seen the large mass redemptions necessary to trigger big taxes of this sort.

3. *Index funds have lower transaction costs.* In an actively managed fund, the fund manager is constantly buying and selling stocks, which means he is incurring transaction costs. With index funds, the fund manager isn't trading stocks. He only sells stock to pay for redemptions by shareholders and only buys stock when new money comes in from shareholders. The typical index fund turns over only about 2 percent of its stocks every year, while a typical professionally managed fund turns over 80 percent.

The lower expenses of index funds means more money in your pocket. Indeed, study after study has shown that index funds almost always outperform managed funds. According to a recent study by Lipper, Inc., which tracks mutual funds, the S&P index funds outperformed all other groups of stock funds in 1998. They also outperformed them in the previous two years, three years, five years, 10 years, and 15 years.

Table 5-1 lists several popular index funds and their expense ratios.

$CROOGE INVESTING TIP #27

Be Aware of Restrictions on Exiting Index Funds
While index funds are one of the greatest innovations for investors in the last 30 years, they do have one huge disadvantage: Nearly all index funds place some restrictions on redemptions. They don't want people switching in and out of the fund, increasing their costs. In fact, a recent study showed that over 300 mutual funds in the United States impose

redemption fees, up 50 percent since 1997. In addition, some fund supermarkets (see $crooge Investing Tip #32), like those run by Fidelity Investments and Charles Schwab, have added redemption fees for anyone who cashes out in less than six months.

Vanguard (1-800-662-7447), for example, discourages telephone switching into or out of its S&P 500 fund by requiring you to document your redemptions with a letter. If there are "excessive" exchanges, you'll be sent a stern letter by the company and lose your exchange privileges. Other Vanguard index funds also impose various redemption restrictions.

Strong Funds (1-800-359-3379) of Milwaukee has a 0.5 percent redemption fee in its Strong Index Fund for shares held less than six months.

T. Rowe Price's (1-800-225-5132) S&P 500 index fund has both a redemption fee (0.5 percent for shares held less than six months) and an excessive trading policy. It discourages trading fund shares held less than 120 days.

Fidelity Investments (1-800-544-8888) has a 0.5 percent redemption fee for shares held less than 90 days in its Spartan Market Index Fund.

Dreyfus (1-800-645-6561) prohibits telephone exchanges in its S&P 500 index fund and imposes a 1 percent redemption fee on shares held less than six months.

U.S. Global Investors (1-800-873-8637) charges $5 per switch in its All America Equity Fund—not bad for large accounts, but a potential problem for small investors. It also has a $3 quarterly account maintenance fee.

It's important to shop around for an index fund (or any mutual fund) that meets your style of trading. Read the prospectuses carefully to find out what restrictions a mutual fund, and especially an index fund, puts on exchanges or redemptions. While some index funds in a family may impose exit charges or other restrictions, others may not. If you're a market timer, then index funds may not be the best choice for you. But if you're a buy-and-hold investor, willing to ride out the dips, then you'll find index funds one of the lowest-cost—and most profitable—methods of investing.

$CROOGE INVESTING TIP #28

Start Your Index Fund Investing With Vanguard Funds

The lowest-cost mutual funds by far are those offered by Vanguard, especially its index funds. They also offer you the most selection, including short-, medium-, and long-term bond index funds and foreign stock index funds. In fact, about two-thirds of all the money invested in index funds in the United States is invested in Vanguard index funds.

Vanguard is ruthless in cutting costs on its index and other mutual funds. If you can choose only one mutual fund family to invest with, then make it Vanguard.

One of my colleagues at Phillips Publishing, Richard Young, editor of *Intelligence Report* and a tightwad in his own right, raves about the Vanguard index funds:

> One of the many areas in which Vanguard has no competition is in its index funds. Oh yes, there are other index funds, but beyond Vanguard, none that merit your consideration. I recently looked at the numbers for a dozen of the biggest index funds. Four of the 12 had nasty front-end loads, invalidating them, and seven of the remaining eight had expense ratios that were too high. Only Vanguard 500 Index makes sense.
>
> Vanguard uses proprietary techniques to invest cash quickly, reinvest dividends, and trade stocks among Vanguard's vast family of funds to save commission costs. Vanguard also looks to cut your taxes by selling the highest-cost stock positions when it repositions the portfolio. You want a Vanguard index fund to be the cornerstone of your portfolio.

Vanguard's FundAccess program is the part of its discount brokerage service that gives you access to thousands of mutual funds, both Vanguard and non-Vanguard. In fact, it's one of only two mutual fund supermarkets where you can buy Vanguard funds with no transaction fee. (The other is Scudder Preferred Investment Plus: 1-800-988-8316.) For

more information, Vanguard can be reached at 1-800-662-
7447, or at www.vanguard.com.

$CROOGE INVESTING TIP #29

Go to This Web Site to Get Free Info About Index Funds
The best Web site for investing in index funds is Index Funds
Online (www.indexfundsonline.com). You'll find extensive,
frank, and up-to-date discussions on every aspect of index
fund investing as well as links to dozens of articles and Web
sites related to index funds. Best of all, it's free.

$CROOGE INVESTING TIP #30

**Buy Managed Mutual Funds That Have a Long History
of Beating the Indexes**
While most managed mutual funds perform dismally against
the index funds, there are a few stellar performers that actually have long histories of consistently beating the indexes.
Mutual Funds magazine has compiled a list of these funds.
From 1993 to 1998, the S&P 500 soared 220 percent. The
following funds did even better. Call them for a prospectus:

- **Enterprise Growth** (1-800-432-4320), with a five-
  year return of 248 percent. Unfortunately, it has a 5
  percent load. But with a performance like that, it might
  be worth paying it.

- **Northeast Investors Growth** (1-800-225-6704), with a
  five-year return of 261 percent—and it's no-load.

- **Value Line Leveraged Growth** (1-800-223-0818), with
  a five-year return of 226 percent—and it's no-load.

$CROOGE INVESTING TIP #31

Look for High-Load Fund Families That Offer Closed-End Funds
A new trend is for fund families that normally charge 5 percent loads to offer closed-end funds on the stock exchanges.

Closed-end funds trade like stocks on the exchanges. As a result, you can buy them through a discount broker for a very low commission (as little as $10 a trade—see Chapter 4). You can also place a limited-buy order below the current ask, so you might get a better deal on the fund. When you buy an open-end fund, you have no choice; you always pay the net asset price plus the load (5 percent or less). Obviously, buying a closed-end fund can save you a lot. Here are several high-load families that offer closed-end funds:

- **Templeton** (800-342-5236): Templeton group of funds normally imposes a maximum load of 5.75 percent on their open-end mutual funds, but their closed-end funds can be purchased at very little cost through a discount broker. Examples include all the Templeton country funds, such as Templeton China (TCH), Emerging Markets (EMF), and Russia (TRF). Of course, you must be alert to the possibility that the Templeton closed-end funds may be selling for a premium over net asset value (more than the value of the underlying stocks in the fund).

- **Alliance group** (800-221-5672) typically imposes a maximum 4.25 percent charge to buy its open-end funds, but you can buy the Alliance All-Market Fund, a closed-end fund that trades on the New York Stock Exchange (symbol AMO), for a small commission through your broker.

- **AIM funds** (800-347-1919) typically charges up to 5.5 percent load on its open-end funds, but AIM offers its Eastern European Fund (GTF) on the New York Stock Exchange.

- **Van Kampen group** (800-421-5666) imposes a maximum charge of 4.75 percent on its open-end funds, but you can purchase its closed-end fund, Van Kampen Senior Income Fund (VVR), through your broker.

$CROOGE INVESTING TIP #32

Use Mutual Fund Supermarkets to Cut the Costs and Complexities of Fund Investing

About 30 discount brokers offer mutual fund "supermarkets," where you can go to buy thousands of no-load funds, often with no (or very low) transaction costs. Such supermarkets:

- Allow you to switch among funds of different families, as well as funds within the same family.

- Consolidate your account statements so you don't get buried in a pile of statements and 1099s at tax time and throughout the year. You receive this information from the fund supermarket rather than from myriad fund companies, making it much easier for you to keep track of your investments. If you like, you can also have your stocks and bonds held at the same brokerage firm.

- Save you money. At some fund supermarkets, over 5000 no-load funds are available, with no loads and no transaction fees. The supermarket also offers other funds with small transaction fees, usually ranging from $25 to $40, with most being on the low end. A few may charge "switch fees," which you pay if you wish to switch within the no-transaction-fee network. However, these are rare and usually run from $25 to $30.

Unfortunately, not all fund supermarkets are created equal. It's important for you to compare them on whatever aspects are important to you. Does the supermarket carry the funds you're interested in with no transaction fee? If it charges a transaction fee for certain funds, how much is it? What is the minimum purchase? It can range from 0 to $5000, depending on the fund supermarket. Does it charge any fees to switch from one fund to another outside of the same family? How many switches are allowed a year? Most fund supermarkets allow an unlimited number of switches, but a few limit you to only two. Are there other restrictions on switching, such as requiring you to hold fund shares for a minimum number of days or months? This usually ranges from 30 to 180 days, depending on the supermarket. What other services are offered—online trading, free research, etc.?

There are other costs you should watch out for. Some fund supermarkets charge account inactivity fees or annual fees if your account dips below a certain threshold. Others charge annual fees to maintain an IRA. Also, costs aren't the only consideration. Some fund supermarkets have terrible phone service. One survey found fund supermarkets that will keep you on hold anywhere from a minute to 22 minutes, waiting to make a transaction or get a question answered.

For some people, convenience, abundance of choices, and speedy service are the most important considerations. For others, cost is. You'll have to read the brochures from each fund supermarket carefully and make some telephone calls to determine which one best meets your needs.

$CROOGE INVESTING TIP #33

Use These Surveys to Find the Best Fund Supermarkets

Finding the best fund supermarket isn't easy. Fortunately, there are several surveys conducted regularly to make it a little easier for you.

Every year, the American Association of Individual Investors conducts a comprehensive survey of fund supermarkets (26 were covered in their 1998 survey) and publishes the results in its magazine, *The AAII Journal*.

In the most recent survey, Dreyfus (1-800-843-5466; www.dreyfus.com) had the most funds available, with a whopping 7015 no-load funds offered that required no transaction fees.

Scudder Brokerage Services (1-800-700-0820; www.brokerage.scudder.com) was second with 6750.

Dead last was Vanguard Brokerage Services (1-800-992-8327; www.vanguard.com), with only 87 no-load, no-transaction-fee funds offered. However, Vanguard is one of only two fund supermarkets where you can buy the ever-popular Vanguard funds without paying a transaction fee.

A smaller firm, Bush Burns (1-800-821-4803; www.bushburns.com) was the leader in the number of no-load fund families offered: 475.

Second was AccuTrade (1-800-494-8946; www.accutrade.com) with 288.

Third was Waterhouse (1-800-934-4443; www.waterhouse.com) with 250. Last again was Vanguard, which only offers one no-load fund family (guess which one), without charging a transaction fee.

Smart Money, in its 1999 survey of 21 discount brokers, picked Ameritrade (1-800-454-9272; www.ameritrade.com), Accutrade, and Waterhouse as first, second, and third best in the rankings for mutual fund supermarkets.

Kiplinger's *Personal Finance* magazine surveyed 22 of the leading fund supermarkets in 1999. According to its rankings, the top supermarket, overall, was that offered by Scudder Preferred Investment Plus (1-800-988-8316; www.scudder.com):

> Scudder offers the most no-transaction-fee, no-load funds, including many low-cost funds, such as Vanguard's. You can consolidate your stock and bond holdings with Scudder, too. It costs $24.95 to trade up to 1000 shares on the Internet. The only downside: You must invest $100,000 with Scudder. If your balance falls significantly below that, Scudder may bill you $125 annually.

Coming in second place in Kiplinger's 1999 survey was National Discount Brokers (1-800-888-3999; www.ndb.com). The two runners-up were DLJdirect (1-800-825-5723; www.dljdirect.com) and Muriel Siebert (1-800-872-0666; www.siebernet.com).

While the results of these surveys vary slightly—because they use slightly different criteria and a slightly different list of fund supermarkets—they give you an idea of which fund supermarkets are among the best. They'll help you narrow your choice to a handful of companies. Then you can call each of these companies (or go to their Web sites), get their literature, and compare each one on the factors that are most important to you.

Charles Schwab One Source: The Granddaddy of Supermarkets

This survey wouldn't be complete if we didn't discuss the first major brokerage firm to offer a supermarket of mutual funds at no extra charge: Charles Schwab & Co. (800-435-4000). It may not have the widest variety of funds in its One Source, but it is the biggest in volume. And there are plenty of funds to choose from. Plus, they have the added advantage of having offices in major cities across the United States.

Another supermarket fund service I like a lot is Jack White & Co. in San Diego, CA (800-233-3411). White has been around almost as long as Schwab in offering no-commission mutual funds, and they have over a thousand funds to choose from. And Jack White has been rated tops many years for customer service.

How do Schwab, Jack White, and other supermarkets offer so many "no-load" funds without commission? They arrange to get paid by the fund itself, up to 0.25 percent of every dollar invested in a fund.

$CROOGE INVESTING TIP #34

Use These Web Sites for FREE, Up-to-Date Info on Mutual Funds

"**America's Mutual Fund Superstore**" is what one Dallas-based online brokerage calls itself. You'll find lots of free info on 7000 mutual funds from 500 different families (www.mutualfundworld.com).

Fabian Investment Resources is one of the oldest mutual fund advisory services. Although there's a charge for many of the services offered, it's a good source of information on the best and worst mutual funds (www.fabian.com).

Find a Fund (www.findafund.com). If you're ever looking for an obscure mutual fund, this is the place to go. You'll also find lots of useful information on mutual funds, including analyses of sector funds (mutual funds that invest in a particular industry), advice for beginners, and statistics galore.

Fund Alarm (www.fundalarm.com) monitors over 2500 funds and warns of those that perform below their benchmarks for the past 12 months. It's only updated monthly, so it won't be very useful if you're a frequent switcher. But others may find it an independent, no-nonsense, fluff-free source of useful information about mutual funds, including news about changes in fund management. The site's chat room and bulletin board draw a lot of people who are unhappy with their mutual funds and want to rant about it.

ICI Mutual Fund Connection (www.ici.org) is the Web site for the Investment Company Institute, the leading trade association for the mutual funds industry. You won't find any hard-hitting investigations or exposés of the mutual fund industry here, but you will find some useful educational resources that you can download for free.

Internet Closed-End Fund Investor (www.icefi.com). For $20 a month (or $120 a year), you can get daily reports on the closed-end fund industry, including charts, profiles, and performance comparisons. If you don't wish to pay the subscription fee, there's plenty of free info on this site, including a discussion forum.

Lipper Analytical (www.lipperweb.com) is one of the two top fund analysis companies. You'll find an abundance of information at its Web site.

Morningstar (www.morningstar.net) is the other top fund analysis company. An independent fund-rating agency, you can subscribe for $9.95 a month and receive daily e-mails, portfolio price updates, and in-depth analysis of some 15,000 funds and stocks. There're also lots of free tools and articles for those who would rather not pay. For example, you'll find several bulletin boards, including Morningstar's popular Socialize board and Vanguard Diehards, which is devoted to Vanguard fundholders.

Mutual Fund Education Alliance (www.mfea.com) gives you information on dozens of no-load funds, including information on fees, minimums, fund types, managers, net asset values, daily price changes, and year-to-date returns, as well as one-, five-, and 10-year returns. One feature allows you to monitor the funds you currently own or build a hypothetical portfolio of funds you may be considering.

Mutual Fund Interactive (www.brill.com) has lots of useful FREE information, including an in-depth guide for beginners. It has a moderated newsgroup that draws over 100 posts a day, plus moderated chat rooms for retirees, investment club members, and market times.

Mutual Funds Encyclopedia (www.dasnet.com) costs $59.95 a year, but it lets you graph the performance of some 10,000 funds. There's also a good search engine for the site that allows you to find funds by category, sector, or performance.

$CROOGE INVESTING TIP #35

Join Schwab's Automatic Investment Plan (AIP)

Charles Schwab, as well as several other brokerage firms, offers an Automatic Investment Plan (AIP) using any of the thousand no-load, no-commission funds. This is an ideal program for investing a specific amount of money each month or quarter (typical minimum for each fund is $250). The money is taken out of your paycheck or checking account automatically each month or quarter, per your instructions. This is a great way to build wealth without hassle. There's absolutely no charge for anything.

Schwab's Automatic Investment Plan is an excellent means to achieve your financial goals—saving for retirement, creating an independent source of wealth, building an emergency fund, or setting up your children's education. I've set one up for myself and my entire family and it really works. Automatically, painlessly, I get richer every month no matter what happens. I'm always shocked when I get my monthly financial statement from Schwab and discover how much money I have in these AIP accounts.

6

THE BARGAIN HUNTER'S GUIDE TO HIGHER INCOME AND CAPITAL GAINS

Conservative investors sleep well.

—*Philip Fisher*

INVESTING IN HIGH-INCOME VEHICLES serves several purposes. First, high-quality bonds can be an excellent hedge in times of uncertainty or panic on Wall Street. During a financial crisis, investors often switch from stocks to bonds to protect their portfolios.

Second, bonds serve as an excellent way to earn regular income during retirement. For Uncle Scrooge and anyone else with substantial wealth, high income can be more important than capital gains. A bird in the hand is worth two in the bush. And the less your broker or fund manager takes out in commissions and fees, the higher the income for you.

Bonds are the traditional source for higher income. They are ideal when interest rates are stable or declining, but they can be a disaster when interest rates and inflation are rising.

Brokerage firms have devised ways to keep commissions very low, and in some cases nonexistent. But beware, you can be grossly overcharged by your broker if you aren't careful. The reason is markups. The markup is the difference between the *bid* price, the price at which brokers will purchase a bond, and the *asking* price, the price at which they will sell that bond to you.

$CROOGE INVESTING TIP #36

Earn High Income and Get Capital Gains Too—If You Buy at the Right Time!

Last year, I spoke at a special income-oriented seminar where the theme was High Income Without Risk. Of course, no such beast exists. There is always risk associated with above-average yields. I told the audience that the secret to success is to wait patiently for extreme conditions in the income market, undervalued situations that offer unusually high yields and the potential for growth.

Such "double win" opportunities don't come along very often. In the past 10 years, I can think of only three cases where we took advantage of such special situations:

1. In May of 1989, I recommended some unique commodity bonds issued by Magma Copper, the second largest copper producer in the United States. These Magma Copper bonds were selling around 90 (below par) and yielding a remarkable 15 percent. What made these bonds unusual was the fact that the coupon yield was linked to the price of copper and could pay as high as 18 percent! Magma Copper issued this strange commodity bond to encourage investors to participate in a leveraged buyout.

Two and a half years later, the bonds were called at 106, giving most of my subscribers a 40 percent-plus return on their money. We were lucky investors.

2. In January 1991, I urged subscribers to buy a junk bond fund named High Income Advantage Trust (NYSE: YLD) at $3½ and yielding an unbelievable 23 percent. YLD was trading at a 20 percent discount from its net asset value because the government forced S&Ls and banks to unload their high-yielding risky bonds as quickly as possible. But one bank's junk is another investor's gold mine—ours!

    Two years later, the closed-end fund was still paying out the same dividend, and the price had soared to $5 or higher. (YLD is still around, but it's not recommended despite its high 11 percent yield. It is selling at a huge premium, 36 percent, over NAV!)

3. During the congressional elections of November 1994, I urged subscribers to vote for VOT—to buy the Van Kampen Opportunity II Fund (NYSE: VOT) at $9⅜. VOT is a closed-end muni fund that at the time was yielding an enticing 9 percent, tax-free. After the Republicans took Capitol Hill, the bond market rallied and VOT jumped to $11. (VOT is still around but no longer a bargain at $12⁵⁄₁₆ and a yield of only 6 percent.)

It's possible to find these double win gems in the income market, but they are rare indeed. To profit, you have to be patient enough to wait for a fallout in junk bonds, emerging market debt, or some other highly speculative income vehicle.

The most recent example, covered in my newsletter, *Forecasts & Strategies,* is the First Australia Prime Income Fund (AMEX: FAX). Historically, First Australia Prime sold at a price as high as $10 a share, but then fell sharply (to under $6) when the Australian dollar came under pressure in the mid-1990s. In early 1999, however, the Australian dollar started to recover, probably a response to the 2000 Olympics coming to Sydney. I first recommended this closed-end fund in December 1998, at $6, and some were able to buy it for less. At the time, it was yielding over 12 percent. Since then, it has risen slightly, in addition to providing a double-digit yield.

Another recent recommendation is Freeport McMoRan's convertible preferred shares that pay an internal rate of return of 12 to 16 percent, with potential capital gains to boot. Freeport (NYSE: FCX), a highly profitable natural resource company, offers three preferred stocks (B, C, and D shares) linked to the price of gold and silver, both at cheap levels that are likely to rise in the next few years. For example, Freeport McMoRan Convertible Preferred B (NYSE: FCX.B) currently pays a $1.02 annual dividend, yielding 5.2 percent. In addition, the preferred B share, which sells for only $19.75, matures at 10 percent of the price of gold (currently $292 an ounce), or $29.20 on August 1, 2003. Hence your internal rate of return is 14.5 percent a year for the next three years! If the price of gold rises (likely), you will earn substantially more.

I suggest you add one of these preferred to your income portfolio, not only as a way to earn a good return but as a hedge against rising inflation. Among the two gold preferreds, my preference is the gold preferred B (FCX.B), which has a shorter maturity but higher internal rate of return than C. The silver preferred D also looks appealing, with an internal rate of return of 17 percent a year until 2006.

What are the risks? First, it's always possible for gold and silver prices to decline further, although I doubt it, given the high level of monetary inflation. Second, Freeport McMoRan Copper & Gold (NYSE: FCX, $19) earns its income from its massive Grasberg copper/gold mine in Indonesia, which could be subject to further political disruptions. It appears that the new government in Indonesia is gradually restoring order there, so I'm optimistic.

Two brokers familiar with Freeport McMoRan's convertible preferred shares are Alex Green at Merrill Lynch in Winter Park, FL, 800-937-0409, and Rick Rule, Global Resource Investments in San Diego, CA, 800-477-7853.

I have an income section in each issue of my newsletter where I offer the latest undervalued opportunities. (Call Phillips Publishing at 800-777-5005 for subscription information.)

$CROOGE INVESTING TIP #37

High Income Investors: Buy an Insured, Closed-End Muni Bond Fund; They're Better than Taxable Treasuries!
For high-income investors seeking tax relief, it's hard to beat the Blackrock Insured Muni Bond Fund (NYSE: BMT), yielding nearly 6 percent, tax-free. As of this writing, BMT is matching the return of Treasuries, even though it is tax-free, an incredible deal.

But remember, BMT invests in long-term munis, so its value can drop sharply when interest rates rise.

$CROOGE INVESTING TIP #38

Boost Your Income With Prime Rate and Floating Rate Funds
I usually don't recommend buying a closed-end fund at a premium over net asset value (NAV). I also usually don't recommend funds that have higher-than-normal expense ratios. There's one exception, however: prime rate funds.

With a prime rate fund, you can earn an income several percentage points higher than the yield on Treasuries, mortgage paper, or money market instruments like certificates of deposit.

Not only that, but you don't have the interest-rate risk. As every first-year economics student is taught, if interest rates rise, the prices of bonds fall. That can be devastating, as many bond investors found out in the 1970s, when interest rates soared to double digits and the price of bonds crashed.

Prime rate funds invest in variable-rate senior loans to corporations at interest rates tied to the so-called prime rate. Even after charging stiff fees of 1.4 percent or more, funds holding these loans are yielding at least 7 percent. Yields on 3-year Treasuries are currently 6.5 percent.

The reason for the high expense ratios? Your fund, to a degree, is acting more like a bank than a bond fund. It has to appraise borrowers' credit quality and take a chance on an investment that is not traded every day and is not liquid. There's a lot more work involved than there is in taking positions in five Treasury notes and sitting on them.

What's the downside? For one, if the prime rate declines, you get declining interest income. Next, there's credit quality. The senior loans are collateralized and go to respectable borrowers, but there are no government guarantees. Third is liquidity. Two funds trade publicly, but the others are redeemable only quarterly.

If interest rates rise, bond funds get hammered. Prime rate funds don't. In fact, they remain remarkably stable. In 1994, when investors suffered terrible capital losses on long-term bonds, Pilgrim America Prime Rate Trust (NYSE: PPR) enjoyed a stable net asset value and delivered more than 7.5 percent total return for the year.

Pilgrim America Prime Rate Trust is the oldest and one of the best of this breed of funds (trading since 1992). I also like the Van Kampen Senior Floating Rate Fund (NYSE: VVR), especially if you can get it at a discount from NAV. VVR invests in a diversified portfolio of senior, fully collateralized bank loans to corporations.

I also recommend various floating rate and foreign income funds, especially if they can be bought below NAV. Among those worth considering are the First Australia Prime Fund (AMEX: FAX), which is a play on the Australian dollar, interest rates, and the economy down under.

You might also look at the Emerging Markets Floating Rates Fund (NYSE: EFL), which invests in dollar-denominated emerging market debt. But this fund is not for the faint of heart. It can be extremely volatile, rising and falling with the fortunes of emerging market debt.

$CROOGE INVESTING TIP #39

Buy Bond Funds or Unit Investment Trusts

The market for corporate and municipal bonds tends to be illiquid. A typical bond may trade 30 or 40 times a day, compared to several thousand times a day for U.S. Treasuries. Ways to keep these markups to a minimum are discussed later in the chapter. The easiest way to buy bonds—and for many investors, the least expensive way—is through a bond fund or a unit investment trust (UIT). The median expense ratio on load (commission) bond funds is 0.93 percent. The median expense ratio on no-loads is 0.80 percent. Obviously, you would want to choose a no-load bond fund.

The Vanguard Group of Mutual Funds (Vanguard Financial Center, P.O. Box 2600, Valley Forge, PA 19482; 800-662-7447) offers a wide range of bond funds with low expense ratios. The average expense ratios on the Vanguard bond and municipal bond funds are around 0.25 percent, well below the averages for bond funds in general. Vanguard has several bond funds to choose from: municipal, Ginnie Mae, government and corporate, with a variety of maturities.

Another low-cost way of buying bonds is through a unit investment trust. In a UIT, you buy an undivided interest in a portfolio of bonds. You will receive a proportional share of the net income of the trust and, as the bonds are sold or mature, a return of principal.

The sales load on most unit investment trusts is high, typically 4 percent. However, the high commission is offset by extremely low management fees (around 0.3 percent). Because unit investment trusts are not actively managed, they generally hold to maturity.

Another advantage of UITs (and individual bonds) over bond funds is that you have a better chance of getting your principal back. Here's why: If you have a bond fund and bond prices drop because of rising interest rates, the bond fund may never recover because it is constantly selling old bonds and buying new ones. (Bond funds do not necessarily hold their bonds to maturity.)

If you have individual bonds or unit investment trusts, you can hold on to the bonds, and they will eventually go back up as they mature.

One more tip: Sometimes you can find great bargains and high yields from closed-end bond funds that trade on the Big Board and the national exchanges. In my newsletter, I've recommended closed-end bond funds issued by Putnam, Van Kampen, Nuveen, and other companies. Some have paid double-digit yields plus capital gains if bought at the right time. Check the latest *Barron's* or *The Wall Street Journal* for a complete list.

$CROOGE INVESTING TIP #40

Try John Nuveen or Van Kampen for a Low-Cost Unit Investment Trust
There are two firms that offer low-cost unit investment trusts: John Nuveen & Co. and Van Kampen Focus Portfolios. Among John Nuveen's current offerings are:

> *Nuveen Defined Portfolios Unit Trusts, Series 41,* which holds a portfolio of U.S. Treasury notes and zero-coupon bonds issued by the U.S. Treasury. They're subject to a maximum sales charge of 1.75 percent. The minimum investment is normally $5000 or 50 units, whichever is less. However, for Education IRAs, the minimum investment is $500, and for traditional or Roth IRAs, it's $1000.

> *Nuveen Defined Portfolios Fixed Income,* which contains both U.S. Treasury securities and corporate

bonds. The corporate bonds are insured to guarantee the scheduled payment of interest and principal, but not the market value. The maximum sales charge is 4.9 percent, and the same minimums apply.

Nuveen Defined Portfolios Insured Corporate Trust invests in a portfolio of insured corporate bonds and has a maximum sales charge of 4.90 percent.

Van Kampen's offerings include:

Municipal bond trusts, which have a range of sales charges from 3.9 percent to 4.9 percent and a minimum investment of $1000, although this may vary, depending on the firm selling the trust. A national intermediate-term municipal bond trust is offered, and it has a sales charge of 2.75 percent.

Van Kampen Insured Income Trust, a portfolio of insured corporate bonds, which has a sales charge of 4.9 percent.

Note that both the John Nuveen and the Van Kampen UITs are not available directly; you must buy them through a broker or financial planner. For information or the name of a broker in your area that sells them, contact:

John Nuveen & Co. Incorporated
333 West Wacker Drive
Chicago, IL 60606
1-800-257-8787; 312-917-7700
www.nuveen.com

Van Kampen Funds, Inc.
1 Parkview Plaza
P.O. Box 5555
Oakbrook Terrace, IL 60181
1-888-832-6848
www.vankampen.com

$CROOGE INVESTING TIP #41

These Web Sites Offer Reams of Free Info on Bonds

Bondagent.com is an online bond broker that offers many freebies, including research tools, a municipal bond primer, a taxable equivalent yield calculator, and rating definitions. Go to www.taxfreebond.com.

The Bond Market Association (www.bondmarket. com), an industry trade group, offers lots of information on both public and private-sector debt instruments. On its affiliated site, (www.investinginbonds. com), you'll find information on municipal bonds, updated daily. Another affiliated site (www.govpx. com) offers daily Treasury bond prices.

Bondsonline offers both paid and free information about fixed-income investments from Reuters, Bridge Information Systems, and Interactive Data. You'll find data on federal, municipal, and corporate bonds, although it's a bit sketchier than some of the other sites listed here. Go to www.bondsonline.com.

If you're interested in **convertible bonds,** bonds that can be traded for a set number of shares of common stock at a specific price, then www.convertbond.com is the place to go. You'll find educational material, announcements about new issues, rates, research, and analysts' reports on this site.

If you're interested in **muni bonds,** one of the best sites is www.emuni.com. There is a $25 charge to use its document retrieval system. Also good is a site with a similar name, www.e-muni.com. It too has oodles of free information on the muni bond market.

Fitch IBCA is an international bond-rating agency. It covers some 1000 banks, 400 corporations, and 50 nations on its Web site. Go to www.fitchibca.com.

Moody's is one of the world's top credit-rating firms, and its Web site offers some of the most comprehensive information on the bond markets. You can also find economic analyses of different industries and general economic forecasts.

$CROOGE INVESTING TIP #42

Seven Ways to Make Sure the Markup Is Fair
Here are several ways to make sure the markup is fair on individual bonds.

- Always ask your broker what the markup or commission is. Your broker may not like this. He or she may try to evade the question, but brokers are required to disclose the markup if you ask. If you can't get a clear answer, go to another broker.

- In most cases, you probably shouldn't pay a markup greater than 5 percent. The National Association of Securities Dealers (NASD) generally considers markups of more than 5 percent to be excessive, but this doesn't stop some brokers from charging fees of 8 percent or more.

- Find out your brokerage firm's policy on bond markups. Some firms have strict rules forbidding excessive markups.

- Compare prices with two other firms. One way to determine the markup is to ask them what price they would pay for the bonds. Then ask what they would sell them for. The difference between those prices is the markup.

- Don't place at-market orders for bonds. This is an order instructing your broker to buy the bond at the market price. If the spread is wide, don't buy right away. Place your order in the middle somewhere until you get a reasonably priced execution.

- Buy bonds with short- to medium-term maturities. Longer-term bonds (10 years or more to maturity) generally carry commissions three to four times higher than those on shorter-term bonds.

- Buy higher-quality bonds. The lower-quality bonds are harder for your broker to sell and consequently have higher commissions, sometimes three or four times higher than those on higher-quality bonds. Quality refers primarily to the default risk. Bonds are rated by several independent services (Moody's is the most popular) on a scale ranging from Aaa (the highest) to D (in default). U.S. Treasury bonds are the highest rated (although sometimes I wonder why, considering some of the federal government's spendthrift tax-and-spend policies). Munis and corporate bonds vary widely in their ratings. Anything with a Moody's rating of Ba or lower is considered speculative.

  Nothing is wrong, of course, with buying lower-quality bonds. I've frequently recommended high-yield (junk) bonds to my subscribers, depending on the economic climate. The interest rates paid are much higher than those paid on Treasuries, but you should be aware of the risks on higher-yield bonds. (*Moody's Industrial Manual* rates bonds and can be found in most libraries.)

$CROOGE INVESTING TIP #43

Buy Bonds on Their Initial Offering

Like stocks, bonds are sold commission-free in their initial offerings. Prices are low because of the huge amount of bonds on the market, and the commissions are paid by the issuer. You also get a prospectus if you buy on the initial offerings. Prospectuses are rarely available to buyers in the secondary market.

$CROOGE INVESTING TIP #44

Don't Bypass Your Full-Service Broker

Bonds are one investment for which a full-service broker may be cheaper than a discount broker. A discount broker may have to go to a dealer first to buy the bond you want. The dealer will charge a markup. Then the discounter will put a commission on it, even if it's a small one, before he or she sells it to you. There's no guarantee that your full-service broker will always be cheaper than your discount broker, but it is always worthwhile to check before buying.

Also, don't assume that just because the broker discounts stock commissions, he or she won't put a markup on bonds. You should always make sure you know both the bid and the ask price, even when buying from a discounter.

$CROOGE INVESTING TIP #45

How to Cut Corners When Buying Zero-Coupon Bonds

Zero-coupon bonds are sometimes called deeply discounted bonds. They pay no interest but mature at their face value ($1000). Because of the time value of money, they're sold at a discount to their face value (value at maturity). The computed interest on zeros accrues at a rate that will make them worth their face value at maturity.

One reason people like them is the enormous leverage potential. A slight drop in interest rates can send zeros soaring in price. They're a great way to speculate on lower interest rates.

You should always consider the risks in buying zeros. First, a rise in interest rates can mean big losses. Second, consider the tax consequences. Even though you don't receive regular interest payments on zeros, the IRS taxes you on the phantom interest as if you had received it regularly. For this reason, many people who hold their zeros to maturity put them into a tax-deferred retirement account, such as an IRA or Keogh Plan, or put them in a child's name to fund his or her education.

Finally, the cost of buying zeros can be horrendous. Commissions and markups on zero-coupon bonds are sometimes much higher than they are on other bonds. The North American Securities Administrators Association and the Council of Better Business Bureaus issued an alert several years ago saying that some brokers were charging a markup as high as 15 percent on zero-coupon bonds. It's imperative that you shop around before buying such bonds.

As a low-cost alternative, invest in a zero-coupon bond fund. The best series is the Benham Target Maturity Trust series, available from American Century Investors (800-4-SAFETY; www.americancentury.com). These are no-load funds with reasonable management fees. A wide range of maturities is available on their zero-coupon bonds. Those with the longest maturities have the greatest profit potential and the greatest risk.

$CROOGE INVESTING TIP #46

Buy Bonds at 10 Cents on the Dollar

One interesting speculative technique is to buy the bonds of bankrupt companies. You can sometimes get them for pennies on the dollar. When Chrysler hovered near bankruptcy in the 1970s, the market value of its bonds plummeted. People who bought Chrysler bonds back then made huge profits as Chrysler turned around in the 1980s. A similar situation happened with the Washington Public Power Supply bonds. Of course, the risk is that the company will default on everything, including the bonds.

If you're betting that a company will turn around after a bankruptcy, you're better off buying the company's bonds than its stock. Bonds are a company's senior security. They are backed by collateral, usually cash or equipment, which is sold if the issuer defaults on an interest or principal payment.

Generally, only bank loans or indebtedness are higher in priority for payment of interest or principal.

Dollar-denominated debt in developing countries has been used as an interesting speculation over the past 10 years. Mexican, Brazilian, and other Latin American bonds have sold at substantial discounts (as low as 30 cents on the dollar), depending on their government's ability to pay. One of the most profitable plays has been to buy debt from developing countries that have recently adopted progrowth, profree market reforms. Examples include Chile, Mexico, and Argentina. Their dollar-denominated debt has increased substantially in value, thanks to a variety of factors: falling interest rates worldwide, greater fiscal responsibility in developing countries, and the fact that many of the dollar-denominated bonds were Brady Bonds, debt from developing countries backed by the U.S. government.

One of my favorite Scrooge investments in 1993 was GT Global High Income Fund, one of the first developing-nation debt funds. It rose 40 percent, including dividends! But emerging-market debt isn't for the fainthearted. In 1994, the fund dropped 19 percent, following the debacle in Mexico. In 1995, it appeared that bargains were again developing in the emerging markets, with yields as high as 26 percent in some dollar-denominated debt. These are the kinds of speculations the bargain hunter is looking for. But they are not for the risk-averse investor.

7

CUTTING THE COST
OF HOLDING CASH

Ready money is Aladdin's lamp.

—*Lord Byron*

VERY FEW INVESTORS are fully invested all the time. New funds are added to a portfolio, and the wise investor may hold these funds in cash waiting for an investment opportunity to come up. Or the Scrooge Investor may sell some stocks from time to time and place the profits in cash temporarily.

Where is the best place to hold cash? One of the most important factors in answering this question is the cost of holding cash. Costs of holding cash usually aren't large, and they may even escape your notice. As all wise misers know, however, those nickels and dimes add up. Benjamin Franklin's popular maxim, "A penny saved is a penny earned," is still valid today. And Franklin was one of the first Scrooge Investors.

You may well recall the cartoon depictions of Uncle Scrooge's vault, filled with gold and silver coins and greenbacks stacked a hundred feet high. Such a hoard makes little sense today! (It is smart, however, to keep a bag or two of gold, silver, and cash in case of a national emergency or a banking crisis.)

$CROOGE INVESTING TIP #47

Don't Hold Too Many Greenbacks

When you hold greenbacks—cold, hard cash—in your possession, the cost is substantial. It is what economists call *opportunity cost,* the amount you give up by not having that money at work earning interest.

If you keep a lot of cash stuffed in a mattress, or even in a safe-deposit box, you're not even breaking even; you're losing money. That's one reason I don't recommend holding anything more than a few thousand dollars in greenbacks. Another reason is that large amounts of cash often serve as a lure for thieves and may even be viewed as a sign of criminal activity, such as drug dealing.

You're far better off keeping most of your cash in an interest-bearing account of some type—even a passbook savings account—than socked away not earning anything. But you can do better than a bank account.

$CROOGE INVESTING TIP #48

Find the Best Bank Rate in Your State

Whether you're shopping for a loan, a CD, or a money market account, you can find the best rates on the Internet. Go to www.bankrate.com. Sign up for their free "Rate Alert" e-mail service, which will keep you abreast of mortgage rates, credit card deals, CD rates, small business finance, and banking issues.

Another source of the best rates for credit cards, mortgages, auto loans, savings accounts, and more is at *Money* magazine's Web site, www.moneycom/rates.

One more great source of consumer information on credit cards is www.cardweb.com, which updates its Web site weekly with news of the credit card industry. If you're a credit-card junkie, bookmark this site and visit it weekly.

$CROOGE INVESTING TIP #49

Get the Highest Bank Rates in Cyberspace

More and more people are stashing their savings in online banks. These are banks that exist largely in cyberspace. They don't have lots of branches, ATMs, tellers, . . . or overhead. The savings are often passed down to customers, and they offer some of the best deposit rates in the country.

Of course, if you're the type who likes talking to tellers or you just feel safer having your money in a bank made of bricks and mortar, online banking is not for you. But these banks are insured by the FDIC, just like any other bank, so they're not fly-by-night operations. If you're comfortable with computers, you can get a half point or so higher interest rate.

My favorite cyberbank is www.everbank.com. It offers the following services:

- FDIC-insured interest-bearing checking account: Current yield is an outstanding 5.25 percent, with absolutely no fees. Even the first 50 checks are free. Minimum balance is $1500.

- No fee VISA ATM debit card: Everbank does not charge a transaction fee, and even rebates up to $4 a month for foreign bank ATM charges.

- Unique VISA credit card: For $69 a year, you get an Everbank VISA card that earns frequent flyer miles with all airlines and no seat restrictions on any flight as long as you book 21 days in advance. No blackout dates or restrictions.

- Mortgage Direct: You can get an immediate approval and rate quote from Everbank's online mortgage service.

For details, see its Web site, www.everbank.com.

Another bank, Salem Five VirtualBanking, offers a checking account with no monthly fee; a WorldAccess MasterMoney debit card, which gives you free ATM transactions; free software; and the ability to download your transaction information to popular personal financial management programs, including Quicken.

You can get almost any service at an online bank that you can at traditional banks, including mortgage lending, online brokerage services, and business equipment leasing services.

Another bank, Net.Bank, even offers online safe deposit boxes! Of course, you can't hoard your gold coins there. You can only store electronic documents, such as tax returns, wills, legal documents, personal files . . . or steamy e-mails that you want to keep private.

Unfortunately, it will be some time before online banking becomes as popular as traditional banking. But if you want to get cheaper loans or higher interest rates, compare the offerings at some of these leading online banks:

Telebank (www.telebank.com)

Net.Bank (www.netbank.com)

Salem Five VirtualBanking (www.salemfive.com)

Security First Network Bank (www.sfnb.com)

$CROOGE INVESTING TIP #50

Chuck Your Checking Account and Get an Unlimited Checking Money Fund

Many banks nickel-and-dime their customers to death on their checking accounts, with minimum fees, ATM charges, insufficient funds fees, and fees for cancelled checks. Even at the cheapest banks, you'll still pay an average of $3.14 a month for a no-frills checking account, $13.00 a month on a basic checking account.

Many consumers are revolting against these charges. They're opening accounts at one of the 80-plus money market funds that offer check-writing privileges.

Unfortunately, most of these funds have minimum amounts for their checks that are so high they can't be used for everyday check-writing. But a growing number are offering services similar to banks, such as ATM cards and debit cards. Some even have no—or very low—minimums for writing checks. The combination of low costs and the high interest rates they offer makes them tempting for a cheapskate.

If your money market fund doesn't offer low-minimum check-writing, look into one of those that does. Here are three you might start with:

> American Express's Strategist Money Market Fund offers unlimited check-writing but charges $2 for each check under $100. Call 1-800-297-7378.

> The money market fund offered by a small mutual fund group, Citizens Funds, in Portsmouth, NH, has unlimited checking and a MasterCard debit card. Annual fee: $35. Call 1-800-223-7010; www.efund.com.

> United Services Fund's Treasury Securities Cash Fund allows you to write as many checks as you want for any dollar amount, if you maintain a minimum balance of $1000. It doesn't offer an ATM card, however. Call 1-800-873-8637.

$CROOGE INVESTING TIP #51

Get the Lowest-Cost, Highest-Yielding Money Fund

Comparison shopping among money market funds can be an incredibly tedious and time-consuming endeavor. There are over 1000 of them, all with different portfolios, expense ratios, checking privileges, tax statuses, and other features. Imagine the difficulty you would have in ordering prospectuses from all those firms, studying them, and plotting the differences.

Fortunately, someone has already done all that for you. Every Monday, *The Wall Street Journal* ($0.75 a copy) lists the latest yields on money market funds.

The most comprehensive source of information on money market funds available is the *IBC/Donoghue's Money Fund Directory.* On the Internet, you can get a free copy of IBC's *Money Fund Report,* a quarterly report that lists the 20 top retail money funds by yield, including government-only money funds, general-purpose money funds, and tax-free money funds. Go to www.ibcdata.com/topper.htm.

$CROOGE INVESTING TIP #52

Invest in Money Funds With Low Expense Ratios

The highest yield funds are generally those with the lowest expense ratios, the ratio that compares mutual fund expenses for management and other overhead to average net asset value.

Expense ratios on money funds can range widely, from 0.30 percent to 1.69 percent. Two of the funds with the lowest expense ratios are WM Money Market Fund (WM Group of Funds, P.O. Box 9757, Providence, RI 02940; 800-222-5852) and Vanguard Money Market Prime Reserves Portfolio (Vanguard Group of Investment Companies, P.O. Box 2600, Valley Forge, PA 19482; 800-662-7447). Their expense ratios are 0.45 percent and 0.33 percent, respectively.

$CROOGE INVESTING TIP #53

Invest in Money Funds That Waive Their Fees

At least two money market funds either partially or fully waive their fees. This is a marketing strategy to draw in customers, but if it saves you money, who cares? The two are the Dreyfus Worldwide Dollar Money Market Fund (Dreyfus Service Corp., P.O. Box 9387, Providence, RI 02940; 800-782-6620)

and the Fidelity Spartan Municipal Money Market Fund
(Fidelity Investments, P.O. Box 626724, Dallas, TX 75262).

As of this writing, Dreyfus has waived its management
fee several times in the past and is likely to do so again.
Fidelity Spartan is waiving its fee only partially, but it still
means a greater yield to you. It guarantees that its management fee will not go above 0.45 percent through the foresee-
able future, one of the lowest available. Of that amount,
Fidelity is currently absorbing all but 0.15 percent. But even
at the full 0.45 percent, it will still be one of the lowest-cost
money funds.

Of course, Dreyfus and Fidelity aren't the only money
market funds currently waiving their fees. They're just the
most widely advertised ones. Other funds may waive their
fees for a time. It pays to watch the advertising in various
financial publications or in the business section of your local
newspaper to find them.

$CROOGE INVESTING TIP #54

Buy T-Bills Directly From Uncle Sam

In general, I dislike investing in U.S. government securities.
As far as I'm concerned, it's money thrown down the drain.
All it does is fund and encourage wasteful government
spending. I much prefer to invest my money in the private
sector, where it's doing some good.

However, there are times when Treasury bills pay slightly
higher rates than bank CDs. They can also give you a big tax-
planning advantage. Treasury bills do not pay regular interest the way a bank or money market account does. Rather,
they are sold at a discount, based on the prevailing interest
rate, and you are paid the full amount at maturity. If the T-
bills you buy today do not mature until next year, you can
postpone taxes on the interest until then. In T-bill money
market funds, interest is generally posted monthly, and it's
taxable in the year you receive it.

If you buy T-bills through a bank or broker, you'll have to pay $35 to $60 for each transaction. If you sell before maturity, you'll pay that amount again. However, you can buy T-bills and other Treasury securities directly from the federal government through the Treasury Direct program, completely eliminating fees and commissions.

Previously, buying Treasury securities direct from Uncle Sam was fraught with hassles. In the last few years, they've made their program a little easier to navigate. They've also made Treasury bills more accessible to smaller investors. Although Treasury bill maturity dates still range from three months to 12 months, the minimum purchase has declined from $10,000 to $1000. Here's how the program works:

1. When you buy, you fill out a "tender" form, whether you're buying bills, notes, or bonds. On the form, you can authorize the Treasury to debit the cost from your bank, brokerage account, or money market fund. The debit is made on the same day your Treasury is issued, so you lose no interest. Just check with your financial institution and find out if it offers the electronic debit option and if it will charge you for it. Some do; some don't. If it does, you might want to pay the old-fashioned way—with a certified or cashier's check.

2. When your Treasury bills are close to maturity, you'll get a notice in the mail telling you they're about to mature. You can roll them over simply by using a Touch-Tone telephone, 24 hours a day. If you don't have a Touch-Tone phone, you can reinvest by prearranging your rollover. However, for automatic rollovers, you must reinvest in the same type of Treasury and in the full amount.

3. To redeem your Treasuries at maturity, you don't need to do anything. If the Treasury doesn't receive any

instructions from you, the proceeds are automatically forwarded to your account.

4. If you want to sell before maturity, it's still a hassle, though not as much as it used to be. You have to mail a form to the Federal Reserve Bank of Chicago. It will get the price quotes from dealers and sell for the highest bid. Two days later, you should have the proceeds in your account. There's a $34 fee to cover the Fed's cost.

For more information on Treasury Direct, call its toll-free number (1-800-943-9864) or go to its Web site (www. treasurydirect.gov). In fact, you can even make your purchases over the Internet.

$CROOGE INVESTING TIP #55

Use Short-Term Funds With a Tax-Advantage Twist

Two short-term funds managed by the Permanent Portfolio Group of Funds (Terry Coxon) offer a unique tax advantage. Coxon manages the funds so that there is little or no tax!

The Permanent Portfolio Treasury Bill Portfolio defers current taxation and thus helps you keep your money out of Uncle Sam's pocket. Like most money funds, it charges no commission and offers check-writing privileges. It invests only in short-term Treasury securities.

Unlike other T-bill funds, however, it doesn't declare a daily dividend. Rather, it reinvests its earnings, so share value increases every day. This means that the earnings you receive are not taxed until you redeem your shares.

It's a clever concept, but it has a few drawbacks. First, you pay a fee of $1.00 for each check you write. Second, there's an account maintenance fee of $1.50 per month. Third, there is an unavoidable startup fee. However, the checks can be any size, and there's no limit on the number of checks you can write in a month.

The Versatile Bond Portfolio Fund is similar, except that it invests in high-grade corporate notes that mature in less than two years. Coxon manages the Versatile Portfolio so that most or all taxes are deferred. The principal tends to vary more than the T-bill fund, but the return is higher. In 1998, Versatile returned 4.82 percent tax-deferred, versus 4.04 percent tax-deferred in the T-bill fund.

These tax-deferred funds are best suited as alternatives to savings accounts for people who maintain large balances in their money funds. They can also be used for estate planning: shares you don't redeem during your lifetime can be passed on to heirs, free of income tax.

For more information, contact the Permanent Portfolio Family of Funds, P.O. Box 5847, Austin, TX 78763; 800-531-5142, or 512-453-7558.

PART 2

THE ONLINE
SCROOGE INVESTOR

8

SCROOGE INVESTING ON THE INTERNET

Better that a man should tyrannize over his bank balance than over his fellow citizens.

—John Maynard Keynes

THE LOWEST STOCK COMMISSIONS YOU'LL FIND are on the Internet. If you have a computer and modem, you can trade stocks for as little as $5 per trade! In fact, you'd be hard-pressed to find a broker who charges more than $30 on the Internet.

But buyer beware! As economist Milton Friedman said, "There ain't no such thing as a free lunch." Delays in having your online transactions processed are common. They can range from a few minutes to a few hours.

Sometimes, too, investors make mistakes. If you key in an extra zero, you might find yourself buying 1000 shares instead of 100 shares. Or you might end up buying when you really wanted to sell. Whatever mistakes you make in online trading, you'll be held responsible for them, and you'll have to pay for them out of your own pocket.

When the markets are moving fast and furious, sometimes computer systems crash. All of the major online brokers have suffered an "outage." If that happens, you won't be able to trade your stocks until the system is back up and running, which could take anywhere from a few minutes to a few days.

These are just a few of the problems with online brokers and trading. Does this mean you shouldn't trade online? Not at all. You can save bundles of money, so why not? Just go in with both eyes open.

Much of the advice in Chapter 4 regarding discount brokers applies to online brokers as well, but with some additional caveats, which you'll find outlined in this chapter.

$CROOGE INVESTING TIP #56

Pay Little Attention to Commissions

This may seem like an odd recommendation, considering that this book is all about saving money. But with online brokers, cost isn't a major consideration. All of them are dirt cheap.

Charles Schwab charges $29.95 for an online trade—and is one of the most expensive. Brown & Co. charges $5, and that is the least expensive. Most of the other online brokers fall somewhere in between.

Charles Schwab, however, offers mutual funds and reams of free research. Brown & Co. is a no-frills broker that offers very little in the way of extras. If you choose an online broker based solely on cost, you may not get the service you want.

$CROOGE INVESTING TIP #57

Consider These Three Factors When Choosing an Online Broker

So cost is only one factor you need to look at in choosing an online broker, and it's not the most important one. Far more important are the broker's accessibility, the range of services offered, and the support provided to clients.

Accessibility.   How long does it take companies to answer their phones? If you call to request information, and you're put on hold for 15 minutes, that's not a good sign. How easy is it to navigate the firm's Web site. If getting through the site is like trying to solve a Rubik's Cube puzzle, then you'd better be careful.

Make no mistake about it, reliability and accessibility are serious problems for online investors. You want a firm that's quick, easy, and reliable to deal with. Sometimes the lower-cost firms are not as readily accessible. You may save money on commissions, but you lose money on the time you spend waiting on the phone, waiting at your computer, or trying to find your way through a byzantine Web site. If that's the case, then you're better off spending the extra money and trading with one of the more reliable firms.

Range of Services.   Competition is hot, Hot, HOT! among discount brokers. That's great news for a Scrooge Investor, because you get more for your money. Discount brokers can't compete on price anymore; they can't get much lower than they are now. So they compete on services.

But here you need to be a discerning shopper. A broker who offers the most services isn't necessarily the broker you should be using. Use the broker that offers the services that you need. If you don't trade mutual funds, then you don't need a broker that offers mutual fund trading. If you're a long-term investor, and not a day trader (which is probably a good idea; see Tip #61 below), then you don't need real-time quotes on stocks. If you get your research through investment newsletters, then you don't need a firm that gives you free online research.

Client Support.   You want a system that's easy to use, and when problems develop (as they inevitably do), you want to be able to get help immediately.

Before you open an account, examine a firm's Web site. Surf around and see how easy it is to navigate.

Some discount firms answer their phones 24 hours a day. With others, you'll be lucky to get through even when the markets are open. Online trading is fine, but there are times you'll want to reach a real live person. The ultracheap online brokers may not have the personnel available to give you such personal attention.

$CROOGE INVESTING TIP #58

The Lazy Person's Way to Find the Best Online Broker

Comparing online brokers can be a mind-boggling ordeal. There are well over 100 online brokers to choose from, with new ones sprouting up nearly every month and existing firms merging, upgrading their Web sites, changing their commission structures, and offering new services.

It's a robust, competitive industry, which is great for bargain-hunting investors but a nightmare if you try to compare them all yourself and pick the best one. Fortunately, you don't have to. Others have done it for you. Best of all, you can get the research for free.

Several popular financial magazines conduct in-depth annual surveys that cover the top online brokers. Every March, *Barron's* ranks over 20 of the top online brokers on several criteria: trade execution, ease of use, reliability, range of services, and cost. *Money* magazine also has an annual survey covering the largest e-brokers, and uses rankings similar to *Barron's:* ease of use, customer service, system responsiveness, products and tools, and costs. *Smart Money* also has a similar survey. Table 8-1 shows which brokers each publication picked for their top five in their most recent survey.

$CROOGE INVESTING TIP #59

Use These Web Sites to Help You Find the Best Online Broker

Several Web sites also compare discount brokers, perhaps the best being the Gomez Advisors Internet Broker Scorecard. The comparisons are far more extensive than the surveys done by the magazines. For example, if you're interested in finding the best online options broker, you can get that from Gomez's Web site. Here are several Web sites that can help you in your search for the best online broker:

TABLE 8-1   How the Financial Press Ranked Online Brokers in 1999

The top five brokers from each survey in order of ranking			
Barron's	Gomez Advisors	*Money*	*Smart Money*
DLJ Direct	E*Trade	Charles Schwab	Muriel Siebert
Discover	Nat. Discount Brokers	Nat. Discount Brokers	Waterhouse
Nat. Discount Brokers	Charles Schwab	DLJ Direct	Quick & Reilly
Web Street Securities	DLJ Direct	SureTrade	Bidwell
Datek Online	Discover Brokerage	Datek Online	Charles Schwab

Don Johnson's Online Investment Services: www.sonic.net/donaldj/

Gomez Advisors Internet Broker Scorecard: www.gomezadvisors.com/

Internet Investing: www.internetinvesting.com

Investment Club Broker Survey: www.iclubcentral.com/brokers/

InvestorGuide—Brokerages: www.investorguide.com/Brokerages.htm

The Motley Fool's Discount Broker Center: www.fool.com/media/DiscountBrokerageCenter/DiscountBrokerageCenter.htm

Smart Money "The Best and Worst of Online Brokers": www.smartmoney.com/si/brokers/online/

WallStOnline: www.wallstonline.com/html/gp3.html

$CROOGE INVESTING TIP #60

Crashproof Your Online Account

Markets crash every once in awhile. That's bad enough. But you don't want your online broker's system to crash as well. Yet, it happens. Almost every major online broker has expe-

TABLE 8-2   The Top 20 Online Brokers

Accutrade: 1-800-882-4887; www.accutrade.com

Ameritrade: 1-800-454-9272; www.ameritrade.com

Bidwell: 1-800-547-6337

Brown & Company: 1-800-822-2021; www.brownco.com

Datek: 1-888-463-2835; www.datek.com

Discover: 1-800-347-2683; www.discoverbrokerage.com

DLJDirect: 1-800-825-5723; www.dljdirect.com

E*Trade: 1-800-387-2331; www.etrade.com

Fidelity: 1-800-544-7272; personal.fidelity.com

Mr. Stock: 1-800-470-1896; www.mrstock.com

National Discount Brokers: 1-800-888-3999; www.ndb.com

Net Investor: 1-800-638-4250; www.netinvestor.com

Quick & Reilly: 1-800-837-7220; www.quickwaynet.com

Charles Schwab: 1-800-435-4000; www.schwab.com

Muriel Siebert: 1-800-872-0711; www.msiebert.com

SureTrade: 1-401-642-6900; www.suretrade.com

Wall Street Access: 1-800-925-5781; www.wsaccess.com

Wall Street Electronica: 1-888-925-5783; www.wallstreete.com

Waterhouse Securities: 1-800-555-3875; www.waterhouse.com

Web Street Securities: 1-800-932-8723; www.webstreetsecurities.com

rienced some system failure, either a failure of the computer system, the Web site, or the phone system.

System outages typically can last anywhere from a few minutes to a few hours. But they strike without warning and can be devastating to you financially if they cause you to miss an important transaction. They're common enough that you need to take some steps to protect yourself.

First, have accounts at more than one online brokerage. If you have two or even three accounts at different firms, then if one company's system crashes, you can trade at least some of your stocks through the other firms. Having more than three accounts will probably be counterproductive, since mastering more than three different online systems can be maddening.

Second, choose a system that offers Touch-Tone telephone trading. Not all firms allow you to trade through your Touch-Tone telephone, but several do. The commission rates are lower than trading through a live broker, but higher than trading online through your computer. If the firm's Web site crashes, the telephone trading system may still work. This gives you another option.

Third, make sure at least one of your accounts is at a firm with a local branch office. Trading with a company hundreds or thousands of miles away is fine when the computer systems involved are humming normally. But when they break down, it can be a nightmare. It will give you tremendous peace of mind knowing there's a local office you can walk into any time and talk to a real person.

Fourth, if your own computer crashes, use a friend's computer or the computer at your local library. Of course, you could also have a second computer. However, if you use the public library's computer, make sure no one is looking over your shoulder when you type in your password. It also might be a good idea to have a second Internet service provider (ISP), just in case America Online, Netcom/Mindspring, or whatever service you normally use goes down.

SCROOGE INVESTING TIP #61

Guarantee That You Won't Lose Any Money Day Trading
Day trading is to Wall Street what blackjack is to Las Vegas: a fast-paced, high-risk game where most people lose in the long run, but a few manage to win big. Some industry estimates I've seen indicate that 50 to 80 percent or more of day traders lose money. Typical day traders make between 50 and 100 trades a day.

There's one surefire way to avoid losing money as a day trader: Don't do it.

To be a successful day trader, you need a stake of $50,000 to $100,000 to start. If you don't have this much money that you can afford to lose, don't even think about it. A wise investor never gambles with his retirement money, rainy day money, or living-expenses budget. If you must gamble, then do so only with money you can afford to lose without it affecting your standard of living.

Here are some other guidelines that may help you succeed at day trading (or speculating in any market):

- Look at your day trading as a job. You'll have to be at your computer terminal before the markets open, every day, and stay there after the markets close.

- Expect to lose money when you first start. The president of one day-trading firm says that in your first six months, you'll lose anywhere from $10,000 to $100,000 or more. If gut-wrenching losses will keep you awake at night, you're probably better off if you don't day-trade.

- The more you trade, the more you'll pay in commissions. Even though commissions for day traders are low, paying 50 to 100 commissions a day can really add up fast.

- Be prepared for some horrendous paperwork when you're figuring out your income taxes. Computing thousands of gains and losses a year can give you fits.

- Be careful of trading on margin. Day trading is risky enough without using leverage.

SCROOGE INVESTING TIP #62

Use These Web Sites for Day Traders

There are several Web sites geared to day trading. Some of these charge for their services, ranging from $19.95 a month to $139.95 a month. Others are free. Some are run by online brokers that cater to day traders.

Avid Trading Company: www.avidinfo.com

The Daily Trader: www.dailytrader.com

Dayinvestor: www.dayinvestor.com

Daytrader's Bulletin: www.daytradersbulletin.com

Daytraders On-line: www.daytraders.com

The Daytrader Toad: www.members.tripod.com/~day-trader/index.html

Elite Trader: www.elitetrader.com

Mkt Traders: www.dtrades.com

Momentum Trader: www.mtrader.com

Pristine Day Trader: www.pristine.com

TradeHard: www.tradehard.com

Trading Systems Network: www.tradingsystems.net

Trading Tactics: www.tradingtactics.com

9

THE CHEAPSKATE'S GUIDE TO UNLIMITED FREE INVESTMENT INFORMATION (ESPECIALLY ON THE INTERNET)

You have before you wealth untold. . . . [t]he best things in life are free.

—*Good News*

RELIABLE INVESTMENT INFORMATION doesn't come cheap. One newsletter on annual reports sells for $12,000 a year. Most of the better investment newsletters are priced at more than $100 a year. Often, this is money well spent. However, as Uncle Scrooge might say, if you can get the information either free or at a cut rate, why pay retail?

$CROOGE INVESTING TIP #63

Tap Into an Almost Unlimited Source of Free Investment Information
One place where you can get almost unlimited information
on investments is your local public library, and in college
towns, the college library often is open to the public.

Virtually all libraries, even the small ones, get *The Wall
Street Journal* and the major business magazines: *Forbes,
Business Week, Barron's, U.S. News & World Report, Money,
Changing Times,* and *The Economist.* My favorite is *Forbes.*
It's the most irreverent and hardest hitting of the group, and
occasionally I have a column in it!

Many libraries also subscribe to the larger investment
advisory services, such as *Value Line* and *Standard & Poor's.*
These are invaluable sources of unbiased information on hundreds of stocks. Sure, they are putting this information online,
but I find it much easier to access information using the
printed word.

An excellent source of information on mutual funds
available in many libraries is *Morningstar Mutual Funds* and
its companion publication on closed-end funds. *Value Line*
has a similar service.

In some major metropolitan areas, libraries subscribe to
a selection of financial newsletters by the top Wall Street and
financial gurus.

Then there are the investment books. With the price of most
hardcover books over $25, you can save a lot of money here.
With interlibrary loan, you can use your local library to borrow
books from almost any library in the country, or the world. Ask
your librarian for details. Interlibrary loan is especially useful
if you're researching an obscure collectible and need to find
everything ever written on it. It's also a real money saver.
Books on art, antiques, and collectibles can cost over $50.

Don't ignore your librarian, who is not only a money saver
but also a time saver. Librarians know their way around the
library and can usually locate a piece of information faster
than you can. What's more, most libraries will answer simple

questions over the phone, if it's something like looking up an address or a telephone number. They're always pleased to help. After all, that's what you're paying your taxes for.

$CROOGE INVESTING TIP #64

Know What Cut-Rate Newsletter Subscriptions Are Available
One firm will arrange cut-rate trial subscriptions to leading financial newsletters. This is an inexpensive way to sample dozens of newsletters and see which ones you like at a price far lower than what you would pay for a trial subscription to even one newsletter.

For a free catalog describing the trial-issue packages available, write to Select Information Exchange, 244 W. 54th St., Room 714, New York, NY 10019; 800-743-9346; or visit its Web site, www.siesite.com.

$CROOGE INVESTING TIP #65

Use the Internet
We are living in the information age. There is now more up-to-the-minute information available to the average investor than ever before. You can turn on the television and get business and financial news 24 hours a day on some cable networks. In some parts of the country, there are radio stations devoted to investments, round-the-clock. The number of investment magazines, newsletters, and other publications has skyrocketed. Huge, often free, investment megaseminars in Las Vegas, San Francisco, New Orleans, London, Johannesburg, Miami, Orlando, New York, and other cities draw thousands of attendees. But the biggest explosion of investment information has been on the Internet.

$CROOGE INVESTING TIP #66

Use One of the Big Five Investment Megasites
There are thousands of investment sites on the World Wide Web. It's not humanly possible to explore all of them. How-

ever, there are five important megasites, and you should become familiar with at least one of them.

These megasites typically offer you the ability to track one or more portfolios of stocks or mutual funds; provide you with charts, quotes, and news alerts regarding the stocks you're interested in; host chat groups and message boards; offer educational material; and provide research on companies. All of them offer substantial free materials and have reasonably priced paid sections where you can get even more information.

Choosing the right megasite boils down to your personal preference. If you're a technical trader, you might prefer a site that offers a lot of charts. If you buy mostly mutual funds, then you'll want a site that focuses on those. If you are a frequent trader, you might want a site that has news alerts.

Online Investor magazine recently surveyed the free parts of the Big Five financial sites. Here's how they rated each of them for their "overall look and feel."

E*Trade	Good
MSN	Fair
Motley Fool	Good
Quicken	Poor
Yahoo!	Excellent

Of course, this is just a measure of the free versions of these Web sites. They may save their best stuff for paying customers. Here are brief sketches of all five.

E*Trade

www.etrade.com

Although this site is sponsored by the largest online broker, you don't have to be a customer to use much of it. Since it's the only site offering free real-time quotes, it's a good site for active traders. There are substantial charts and fundamental research available on individual stocks. You can also download prospectuses from some 4300 mutual funds.

Microsoft Investor

www.investor.msn.com
While Microsoft Investor (MSN) has lots of free information, you'll have to pay $9.95 a month to get the better fea-
tures, like insider trading data, Zack's earnings estimates,
and *Value Line* fund reviews. For those who like charts,
MSN's free charting feature is one of the best. The Portfolio
Manager, which will help you keep track of your profits and
losses on your stocks and bonds, is also free.

The Motley Fool

www.fool.com
This site reflects the iconoclastic personalities of its popular
founders, David and Tom Gardner, who write frequent com-
mentaries, which are available on the site. It's somewhat weak
on charts, research, and the real facts about individual companies—sometimes they deserve the designation "fool"—but it's
strong on entertainment value (the site's motto is *educate,
amuse, enrich*). You won't find much material on mutual
funds, except for index funds, a favorite of the Motley Fool.
There are message boards, which are monitored by some of the
site's writers. You can ask a question and get an answer. There's
also a portfolio manager where news, messages, charts, company information, and SEC filings are just a click away.

Quicken

www.quicken.com
One of the biggest benefits of this site is the free alert you
get when there's news about or a sharp price change in a
company in your portfolio. The portfolio manager can help
you evaluate your overall portfolio on such factors as asset
allocation and risk, and your individual stocks on such factors as price/earnings ratios, price to sales, market capitalization, and dividend yield. Quicken has a research tool that
gives links to articles that have appeared about any company
you own or you're investigating.

Yahoo!Finance

www.quote.yahoo.com

Yahoo's financial Web site gives you more news sources than any of the others—Associated Press, Reuters, PR wires, Wired, and CBS Marketwatch. You can create as many portfolios as you want of whatever size you want. Its many message boards are quite active, but none of them are actively monitored, so the quality of information is poor. *OnlineInvestor* rated the site as the overall best of the Big Five.

$CROOGE INVESTING TIP #67

Beyond the Big Five, Seven Other Great Web Sites Offer Tons of Free Information

There are several other big Web sites worth visiting. Some of them are equal to the Big Five in terms of the features they offer, and you could just as well use some of these as your main investment info portal to the Internet.

1. **Bloomberg** (www.bloomberg.com) gives you up-to-the-minute market news as well as columns from its regular writers. The site is primarily free, although some parts require a subscription. For most investors, though, the free material will be sufficient. You'll find good coverage here of the world markets, foreign currencies, municipal bond yields, the most active gainers and losers, mutual fund news and announcements, and basic company profiles and charts.

2. **CBS MarketWatch** (www.cbs.marketwatch.com) is a free site that provides you with much the same type of news as Bloomberg's, although not quite as extensive. However, you'll also find discussion boards to suit almost any investment interest you might have.

3. **Morningstar** (www.morningstar.net) is perhaps one of the most useful of these Web sites. It has both free and fee-based sections, the latter only $9.95 a month.

In fact, for the mutual fund investor, this is probably the best site. Some 6500 funds are screened, using 10 screening variables.

You'll find economic news, market updates, fund and stock movers, and other great features. You can track up to 10 portfolios, with 50 selections per portfolio. There's great research that includes 300-plus elements for stocks and 100-plus elements for mutual funds. About 8000 stocks are covered on the site.

4. **SmartMoney.com** (www.smartmoney.com) uses data provided by Dow Jones, and the fund analysis ranks with the best you'll find on the World Wide Web. You'll find a basic portfolio manager with news links, articles on companies, foreign and domestic news, and investment basics.

5. **TheStreet** (www.thestreet.com) gives you free market summary and educational information. However, you'll have to pay about $100 a year if you want certain customized services, such as e-mail updates.

6. **Wall Street City** (www.wallstreetcity.com) also has both free and fee-based features. The site is known for its charting capabilities. The costs vary, but count on spending about $40 a month to access the best features of this site.

7. **Stockscape.com Technologies** (www.stockscape.com) offers over a dozen free investment newsletters, plus top-notch interviews with major investment gurus.

$CROOGE INVESTING TIP #68

These Useful Specialty Sites Give You Free Info That You Probably Can't Find Anywhere Else

Securities & Exchange Commission (www.sec.gov) is the site of the government agency that regulates the securities business. You can go here to search for

prospectuses and other filings from publicly traded
U.S. companies and mutual funds. It's one of the
first places to go if you're researching a particular
company. Like most "benefits" the government provides, it is not user-friendly.

FreeEDGAR (www.freeedgar.com) is another good
place to get these government filings. This is a free
site provided by the private sector, and it's easier to
use than the SEC's site, with much the same information, albeit slightly delayed.

Nasdaq-Amex (www.nasdaq-amex.com): If you're trying to find out information about a small-cap stock
that trades either on the American Stock Exchange
or the Nasdaq over-the-counter market, this is the
place to go. You can get SEC filings, chart the company's price, learn about the company's fundamentals, and find news reports here.

Market Guide (www.marketguide.com) is known for
its excellent snapshots of thousands of publicly
traded companies. You won't find any portfolio
management/tracking capabilities or mutual fund
info—just good, solid, FREE information.

Big Charts (www.bigcharts.com) does just what you
would expect: it gives you great charts.

$CROOGE INVESTING TIP #69

Consult the Two Major Magazines for the Online Investor

The Internet is expanding so rapidly that it's difficult to keep
on top of all the investment sites. Two magazines are being
published that help put the online investing world into per-
spective.

Money.com, a spinoff of *Money* magazine, is the more
general of the two magazines, with features, news items, and
Web site reviews on saving money and investing via the Inter-

net. You'll find articles like "Buying a Home Online," "College on the Internet," "How Online Brokers Fared on Crash Day," and "Buying Cars on the Cheap." It's published monthly, except in November, when it is semimonthly. Subscriptions are $39.95 a year. Contact 1-800-633-9970; www.money.com.

OnlineInvestor is focused more on investing than on general financial and consumer topics. In it, you'll find articles like "The Novice's Guide to Day Trading," "Top Financial Web Sites," and "When Brokers Go Bad: What to Do." Subscriptions are $14.95 a year. Contact info is 1-800-778-8568; www.onlineinvestor.com.

$CROOGE INVESTING TIP #70

Eleven Steps to Ferreting Out False Info From Internet Fraudsters and "Internuts"

Just as the Internet is a great source of information for investors, it is also a great source of misinformation, unfounded rumors, unreliable gossip, overblown claims, and outright lies. You sometimes find this kind of bad material on some of the sites listed above.

The speed and anonymity of the Internet make it an ideal breeding ground for fraudulent stock promotions. The SEC receives 200 to 300 complaints a day about Internet message boards. These are forums geared toward specific areas of the market where anyone can post a message saying anything they like. Professional stock manipulators have learned to use these boards to move a stock thousands of percentage points a day, simply by posting false information which is gobbled up by gullible investors looking to make a killing.

Typical is the "pump and dump" scheme, in which promoters push up a stock's price through false claims, and when the price peaks, unload their shares to the duped investor. They do this through junk e-mail, online newsletters, message board postings, and Web sites filled with false information.

In one of the more clever schemes, the perpetrators fraudulently promoted a high-tech stock by posting a phony news story that was made to look exactly like a real news story, including dedicated links to Bloomberg, the well-respected financial news service.

So how do you separate truth from fiction when the sleazy promoters will go to such extraordinary lengths? Here are a few guidelines to follow:

- Never base any investment decision solely on information you've received, unsolicited, on the Internet.

- Don't believe anything you read on the Internet unless you can confirm it, independently, with at least one other source.

- Insist on receiving financial reports for any potential investment, or better yet, get those reports yourself directly from the sources listed elsewhere in this chapter.

- Be especially careful of investing in those companies that have little or no current income or that have no product or service.

- Be wary whenever you hear certain buzzwords, clichés, or exaggerations, such as "safer than a CD," "the next Microsoft," "sure thing," "ground-floor opportunity," or "inside information."

- Beware of "free stock" offers. These stocks will probably never be worth anything, but to get them, you have to give a lot of personal information that is valuable. You never know where this information will end up.

- Be especially careful of stocks trading for less than $5 a share. The lower the price, the riskier they are, and the more likely it's a promotion scheme.

- Never give a stranger your name, address, or phone number over the Internet. You'll be hounded forever by sleazy promoters.

- Never assume that people are who they claim to be. Always verify credentials (see tip #71, below).

- Read disclosure statements on Web sites and online newsletters. If the fine print says that the Web site or newsletter publisher receives compensation or has a position in the stocks recommended, then you'll have to take everything with a grain of salt. But even if there's no such disclosure statement, you still shouldn't let your guard down.

- If something seems too good to be true, it probably is. Successful Scrooge Investors know that another opportunity will always come along if this one doesn't pan out.

$CROOGE INVESTING TIP #71

Use the Following Nine Web Sites to Check Out Suspect Brokers, Promoters, and Investments

1. **Certified Fraud Examiners** (www.bham.net/users/ jwrhymes/fraud/fraud.html): Although this Web site is run by the Alabama chapter of Certified Fraud Examiners, it's useful for anyone, anywhere who thinks she or he may be the victim of a scam proposal. You'll find links to several other federal, state, and private agencies.

2. **The Federal Trade Commission** (www.ftc.gov) will alert you to whether or not the government's Federal Trade Commission has taken any action against a firm.

3. **Internet Fraud Watch** (www.fraud.org/ifw.htm) gives you tips for avoiding scams and warnings about some of the most common types of scams, including pyramid schemes, credit fraud, and sweepstakes.

4. **Investment Protection Trust** (www.investorprotection. org) is a public service site with good links and educational material on spotting scams.

5. **KnowX** (www.knowx.com): For $1.50 per name and category searched, this site will tell you whether or not a particular business or individual is the subject of any lawsuits, bankruptcies, judgments, or tax liens.

6. **National Association of Securities Dealers** (www.nasd.com) is the Web site for the securities industry's self-regulatory organization.

7. **National Futures Association** (www.nfa.futures.org/ menu.html) has a Disciplinary Information Access Line that can tell you if any disciplinary action has been taken against a particular broker.

8. **Securities & Exchange Commission** (www.sec.gov) gives you documents filed by public companies with the SEC. You can compare these against the claims made by brokers and promoters on the Internet.

9. **Stock Detective** (www.stockdetective.com) warns investors away from "stinky stocks" that are heavily promoted on the Internet.

$CROOGE INVESTING TIP #72

Go to These Message Boards for the Latest Gossip on Hot Stocks

Now that you've been warned about the dangers of message boards, you can learn about the benefits. Gossip moves stocks, especially the hot high-tech stocks. Not everyone lurking on message boards is a promoter or know-nothing amateur. Many mutual fund managers and professional traders use them to keep abreast of the latest gossip on stocks. You can occasionally come across information from insiders. You can get a feel for the market for a particular stock by monitoring what people are saying about it. Just make sure you apply plenty of common sense and skepticism to what you read.

That said, here are four of the most popular message boards:

Motley Fool (www.fool.com) is a free site that allows anonymous posts. But the site is monitored by the staff, so the posts are more focused and the conversations more civil than some of the other sites. There seems to be more focus on the larger stocks than the small-caps. This is not to say you will find out the truth about what's going on, but it is a popular source of gossip. The Motley Fool is sometimes foolish and always motley. Managing people's money is never something that should be treated lightly.

Raging Bull (www.ragingbull.com) is similar to the Motley Fool site but with more discussion of small-cap and penny stocks.

Silicon Investor (www.techstocks.com) focuses on the technology stocks, as the name implies. You can read the messages for free, but to post, you have to be a subscriber (which costs $60 for six months). The quality of the information, though, seems to be somewhat higher than on the free sites where anyone can post messages.

Yahoo!Finance (quote.yahoo.com) is the biggest message board site—and probably the most unreliable. You'll have to search hard to find any valuable nuggets among all the nonsense.

$CROOGE INVESTING TIP #73

Make the Most of "Free" Money Shows and Investment Seminars
Investment seminars are attended by thousands in major cities like San Francisco, Las Vegas, New Orleans, Orlando, and New York City. They can be enormously valuable—or an outright danger—depending on how you use them.

A seminar gives you the opportunity to speak personally with your favorite investment guru, mutual fund manager, financial writer, or stock promoter. You can meet the speakers, get a feel for the personality of the individual, ask tough questions, talk to other investors, compare products among exhibitors, and have a nice vacation.

On the other hand, you might come away from the conference worn out, confused, and paralyzed by the mass of contradictory advice and endless sales pitches. Or you may make an impulsive decision, based on some promoter's glib presentation. Here are five steps you can take to make the most of the money meetings.

1. *Have some idea of what you want from the seminar before you go.* Think of your own needs and goals before you go. Are there specific questions you want answered or specific speeches or workshops you want to attend? Many people go to seminars expecting to be led by the hand to everything. Get a copy of the seminar schedule ahead of time and plan out your strategy. Have three or four specific things in mind that you want to accomplish.

2. *Preplan the event from the moment you get your seminar schedule.* Some people try to do too much at a seminar. If you attend with a spouse or a friend, you can divide the schedule up and attend events separately, especially if there are two events scheduled at the same time.

Usually, tapes are available of specific speeches or workshops. Be aware, however, that not everything is taped. Find out ahead of time which seminars and speeches are being taped and which are not. You can also make friends with others at the seminar. Bring an inexpensive tape recorder and ask another attendee to tape a session for you if you can't attend it. Offer to do the same for that person.

Make sure you save some time at the seminar to have fun. Do some sightseeing. It's good to plan your trip so that you arrive a day ahead of time and leave a day after the conference has ended.

3. *Realize that everyone speaking or exhibiting at a seminar is there to sell you something.* Sometimes all they're selling are subscriptions to their newsletters. Other times they are selling high-priced products like insurance, living trusts, mutual funds, or money management services.

Sometimes the sales pitches are hidden, so you have to listen carefully and try to read between the lines. For example, a newsletter editor who may seem impartial could be using his speech to promote penny stocks that he has a position in. Don't be afraid to ask a presenter point-blank if she owns the stocks she's promoting or if she's received any compensation from the companies she's recommending. Get an independent evaluation of the investment by talking to other experts at the conference or by using the resources listed elsewhere in this chapter when you get home.

4. *Be a wary buyer.* Most of the firms that rent exhibit booths are given only a cursory screening by the seminar sponsor. I've seen many popular speakers and exhibitors at seminars turn out to be crooks. Just because a particular firm has been allowed to exhibit, don't assume it has the endorsement of the seminar sponsor.

5. *Don't make any major investment decisions at the conference.* Let some time pass before you take action on any recommendations. Take a couple of weeks or so to reflect; check banking and other references; examine sales literature, prospectuses, and client account agreements; and sort out the pros and cons. Make follow-up calls to the promoters with your questions. You may want to get a second or third opinion from your own attorney, tax accountant, stock broker, or financial planner.

$CROOGE INVESTING TIP #74

Attend Investment Conferences Sponsored by These Firms
I've attended and spoken at all the investment conferences recommended below. Some are free, others are expensive, but they are all worthwhile.

- **Atlanta Investment Conference:** Held annually in the spring, this three-day conference attracts some 20

speakers and more than 500 investors. The 13-year-old
conference is organized by Martin Truax, the well-
known investment expert from Smith Barney in
Atlanta. The cost is $199–$399, depending on when
you sign up (early birds get a discount), and your
spouse can go at half price. For more information:
Atlanta Investment Conference, 3091 Greyfield Trace,
Marietta, GA 30067; 1-800-864-0014 or 770-859-
9937.

- **International Investment Conferences** holds seven or
  eight big conferences every year, including the Northeast Investment and Money Conference (New York),
  LIFExpo (Anaheim), Investing in the Americas
  (Miami), Western Investment & Mining (San Francisco), and Las Vegas Investment & Mining. It also
  holds several foreign conferences, including Investing
  in African Mining (Indaba, South Africa) and Global
  Emerging Markets (London). The U.S. shows attract
  thousands of investors, primarily because of the tons of
  free tickets given away by mutual funds and newsletter
  editors. For the few who can't wangle a free ticket, the
  cost is only $40 (half price for senior citizens). The
  conferences are sponsored by International Investment
  Conferences, which has held well over 60 such
  shindigs in the last 13 years. For more info: International Investment Conferences, 6310 Sunset Dr.,
  Miami, FL 33143; 1-800-282-7469 or 305-669-1963;
  www.iiconf.com.

- **Intershow** has been giving investment conferences for
  21 years, attracting up to 10,000 attendees and offering
  at least a couple hundred exhibitors and workshops.
  Shows include the San Francisco Money Show, the
  Florida Money Show, the New York Technology Investment Conference, the Las Vegas Money Show, the San
  Francisco Money Show, and the Portfolio Management

Symposium (San Francisco). Admission is free, except for the New York conference. The firm also sponsors Investment Cruises, but you'll pay big bucks for these. Of course, you'll be able to attend the investment seminars on world-class luxury cruise ships and visit exotic ports of call. Write or call Intershow, The Githler Center, 1258 North Palm Avenue, Sarasota, FL 34236; 1-800-970-4355; www.intershow.com.

- **Jim Blanchard's New Orleans Investment Conference:** Jim Blanchard, who pioneered the investment conference back in 1974, passed away in 1999, but his four-day investment extravaganza lives on. His conferences regularly draw several hundred to several thousand investors and have over 40 speakers and some 65 workshops, roundtable discussions, and corporate presentations. They're more expensive than some of the other money shows but still well worth attending. The cost is $595 for the first person and $300 for each additional person. Write or call Jefferson Financial, Inc., 2400 Jefferson Highway, Suite 600, Jefferson, LA 70121; 1-800-648-8411.

PART 3

THE NONTRADITIONAL SCROOGE INVESTOR

10

CUTTING YOUR FEES ON OPTIONS AND FUTURES

No profession requires more hard work, intelligence, patience, and mental discipline than successful speculating.

—Robert Rhea

OTH STOCK OPTIONS AND COMMODITY FUTURES can reduce your risks or increase your leverage and potential profits. They also can be confusing and complicated. But for sophisticated investors they are important tools. Writing a call option on your favorite stock can reduce your risk and give you additional income. Buying a put option on the S&P 100 can hedge your portfolio against a bear market. And so it goes.

Commissions and fees have dropped considerably in options and futures, just as they have in securities, but option and commodity trading can still be extremely expensive if you trade frequently. A growth stock may be held for years, but options and futures contracts are inherently short-term; they are bought and sold frequently.

Commissions at the full-service firms can reach $50 to $100 per contract. *Churning*—excessive trading by brokers to generate commissions—is sometimes a problem with smaller outfits.

Even if you have an honest broker and know what you're doing, you can still lose your shirt because of the powerful impact of leverage. For as little as $5000 (the minimum account size at many firms), you control a $50,000 or $100,000 contract. Your profit potential is magnified 10 to 20 times. But remember, just as your profits are leveraged, so are your losses. A slight move against your position could wipe you out, resulting in a margin call and big losses.

Buying options is usually considered more conservative, or should we say less speculative, than commodity trading, because you can't get a margin call buying options (though you can when selling options). In any case, I recommend that you educate yourself as thoroughly as possible. There are some excellent books available on both topics at your local bookstore or at Amazon.com. And, of course, there's no better education than experience.

$CROOGE INVESTING TIP #75

Use These Resources for Free or Low-Cost Information on Trading Futures and Options

You can get free information on the major option and commodity exchanges. The best source is the Chicago Board of Trade, which trades both options and futures. Check out its Web site, www.cbot.com.

The *Chicago Board Options Exchange* (www.cboe.com) is a great resource for options investors. You'll find an options calculator, quotes from the trading pits (20-minute delay), free e-mail alerts, and several free mailing lists on options.

You can check out any commodity fund through the *National Futures Association* (*NFA*), 200 West Madison St., Suite 1600, Chicago, IL 60606; 800-621-3570; in Illinois, 800-572-9400; www.nfa.org. NFA is a self-regulatory organization. It can verify whether commodity brokers or commodity fund operators are properly registered and whether any disciplinary action has been taken against them. The NFA offers useful booklets and other information on trading commodities, and best of all, it's free:

Derivatives Strategy, a monthly magazine, sponsors a helpful Web site. You'll find lots of educational information about derivatives, including entertaining, comic-book-style explanations of complex trading schemes. Articles from the magazine are archived three months after publication. Go to www.derivatives.com.

FAQs About Futures (www.ilhawaii.net/~heinsite/FAQs/futuresfaq.html) is a good Web site for budding futures traders. There's lots of free educational data, plus links to other useful Web sites.

Futures.Net (www.futures.net) has substantial free global news and market commentary, updated daily.

Futures Magazine is the best source of information on futures and options. It offers books, videotapes, and seminars on trading strategies. Call for a free catalog (1-800-601-8907 or 815-734-1166). You'll also find over 2000 titles on futures and options trading at its Web site, www.futures-mag.com.

INO Global Markets, designed for experienced futures traders, has charts, options tables, and graphs galore. Go to www.ino.com.

The *Options Industry Association*'s Web site is designed by the options industry to promote trading. You can get a free videotape, free software, and information on free seminars and workshops, nationwide, on trading options. Go to www.optionscentral.com.

Schaeffer's Investment Research gives (www.option-source.com) educational materials and daily market analysis on options trading. You can also get a free three-week trial subscription to a newsletter, *Schaeffer on Options.*

$CROOGE INVESTING TIP #76

Use Low-Fee Commodity Funds

Most people are better off investing in commodities through a professional manager. Make sure, however, that you're paying a reasonable fee. Commodity funds are notorious for charging outrageous fees and commissions—up to 20 percent annually.

There are many commodity funds to choose from, but I like Salomon Smith Barney's SB Diversified Futures Fund. The fund consists of four leading advisers. They are reviewed quarterly, and an adviser who is trailing is replaced by a better-performing adviser. Over the past five years, the fund has averaged an annual rate of return of about 20 percent after all commissions and fees.

SB Diversified Futures Fund will invest in all financial and futures markets: stock indexes, interest rates, currencies, the metals, energy, and agricultural commodities. Thus, you get maximum global diversification in all investment markets and maximum manager diversification. You can expect some volatility, however.

If you were to invest directly with any single one of its advisers, you'd probably need a million-dollar minimum. The minimum investment in this fund, however, is only $5000 ($2000 for IRAs). There are no front-end or back-end loads, and you can add to your account on the first of each month and withdraw your funds each quarter. The management fees are typically 1 percent per quarter, plus 15 percent of all profits each quarter (the same that a typical adviser might charge on a million-dollar account).

To take advantage of this futures program, contact any Salomon Smith Barney broker or call Martin Truax at Salomon Smith Barney in Atlanta: 800-425-1071 or 770-393-2000; fax 770-393-1855.

Managed Commodity Accounts

Many commodity brokerage accounts also offer individualized managed commodity accounts. Be sure to check out all

the costs and profit-sharing involved. Even discounters
sometimes offer managed accounts, such as Lind-Waldock
(see Table 10-1).

$CROOGE INVESTING TIP #77

Use Discount Commodity Brokers

If you want to go it alone in commodities, you might consider discount commodity brokers. Like discount stockbrokers, these firms won't give you any advice or hold your
hand through the scary times, but they will give you fast,
efficient, and courteous service and execute your trades.
Some offer managed accounts, too.

Table 10-1 compares the commission charges of the
major commodity discount brokers.

All of the prices are for full-size contracts, based on
round turns. Different commissions may apply if you trade
smaller contracts on the MidAmerica Commodity Exchange
(MIDAM). If you are doing sophisticated strategies, such as
spreads, combinations, butterflies, or boxes, you should

TABLE 10-1   Comparison Survey of Major Commodity Discounters

Firm	Intraday Trade	Overnight Trade	Options	Account Minimum
First American Discount Corp. www.fad.com 800-621-4415	$25	$30	$30	$5000
Ira Epstein & Co. www.iepstein.com 800-284-6000	$26	$30	$35	$5000
Jack Carl Futures www.jackcarl.com 800-621-3424	$25	$30	$35	$5000
Lind-Waldock www.lind-waldock.com 800-445-2000	$25	$30	$35	$5000

check to see what the commissions are. Many firms also charge extra for exchange fees, which run $1 to $3 per contract. Many firms offer free charts, newsletters, and hotlines.

You must be cautious in choosing a futures broker because there is no government insurance to protect your funds if a firm goes under. Make sure the firm you choose has been in business for at least five years, preferably longer. All of the firms listed in Table 10-1 meet this criterion.

When dealing with a commodities broker, you should make sure that any profits you make above and beyond the margin requirements are held in a segregated money market account. That way, you'll be protected if the trading company collapses. Also, make sure that all the cash in your account is earning interest at a competitive rate.

$CROOGE INVESTING TIP #78

Trade Commodities and Commodity Options Online

You can cut your costs even further with discount commodity brokers by choosing a broker that offers online trading. Such firms also offer other free benefits, such as online research and the ability to place orders and get real-time price quotes, 24 hours a day, online.

There are dangers, however. If the system crashes, you can't execute a trade, and you lose money, the brokerage firm is not responsible for your losses. Moreover, because of the volatility and high leverage of commodities, trading them online can be perilous.

Still interested? Check out NetFutures, where you can trade a commodity futures contract for as low as $9.99, less than half of what you might pay to trade through a live discount commodity broker on the telephone.

Of course, all of the major discounters listed in Table 10-1 offer online trading as well. My favorite is Lind-Waldock in Chicago.

$CROOGE INVESTING TIP #79

Search Out the Lowest-Cost Discount Broker for Stock Options

Discount stockbrokers, which were covered in-depth in Chapter 4, also offer discounts on stock options. Commissions on options can vary tremendously. For example, the commission for trading 10 contracts @ $2.00 can range from $17.50 to $68, depending on which discount broker you use.

To make matters even more complicated, not all brokers offer equal services. For example, some brokers may offer good rates on options but insufficient choices in mutual funds. Others may offer poor rates on options but lots of online research reports or an easy-to-navigate Web site.

One of the best resources for finding an online broker for options is through Gomez Advisors (www.gomez.com). This Web site evaluates more than 50 discount brokers quarterly and compares them on the basis of their rates and other qualities. It's the most extensive rating system I know of for evaluating brokers selling options. There's also some good educational information on this Web site for trading options.

11

SAVING MONEY ON PRECIOUS METALS AND BARGAIN HUNTING FOR MINING STOCKS

> All that glitters is not gold.
>
> —*William Shakespeare*

I F THERE IS ONE TYPE of investment that is most precious to Uncle Scrooge, it is gold and silver. He loves his bags of old coins in the money bin. He bathes in it! It reminds him of his roots as a gold prospector. He also keeps three cubic acres of gold and silver because he knows they are the only real money. Like Uncle Scrooge, I recommend that you keep a few bags of coins around. You never know when the government is going to wreak havoc in the economy, and you know how crisis affects the yellow metal: It goes through the roof.

Unfortunately, precious metals investors are routinely overcharged, which is surprising considering how easy it is to save money.

$CROOGE INVESTING TIP #80

Choose From Six Low-Priced Dealers

For years, *Silver and Gold Report* anonymously surveyed some 25 of the country's precious metals dealers to see which ones had the lowest prices.

The savings can be tremendous. The surveys regularly showed price differences of well over $1000 for investments such as 1000 one-ounce silver Canadian Maple Leafs or 20 one-ounce gold coins, such as South African Krugerrands. By taking a few minutes to shop around, you can save hundreds, if not thousands, of dollars.

I've been following this survey for several years. Although the newsletter is no longer in business, many dealers still are, and a handful seem consistently to have the lowest prices in most categories:

- American Century Brokerage, 1665 Charleston Rd., Mountain View, CA 94043; 800-447-4653 or 415-965-4275; www.americancentury.com.

- Camino Coin, P.O. Box 4292, Burlingame, CA 94011; 800-348-8001 or 650-348-3000.

- Dillon Gage, Inc., 15301 Dallas Pkwy., Suite 200, Addison, TX 75248; 800-537-2583 or 972-788-4765.

- Sam Sloat Coins, Inc., 606 Post Road East, Westport, CT 06881; 800-243-5670 or 203-226-4279.

- Silver Towne, 120 East, Old Union City Pike, Winchester, IN 47394; 800-788-7481 or 765-584-7481.

$CROOGE INVESTING TIP #81

Comparison Shop Among Top Coin Dealers

It isn't wise to pick just one coin company and buy from it. You should call at least three companies, preferably all six, one right after the other, to get quotes. Also, a coin dealer may have a low price for one item and a high price for another.

Always ask for the total amount you must pay, including all charges, rather than just getting per-ounce, per-bag, per-bar, or per-coin quotes. Otherwise, some dealers may give you a low quote and then tack on all sorts of charges for commissions, shipping, and insurance.

$CROOGE INVESTING TIP #82

Buy the Lowest-Premium Gold Coins
If you're investing in gold bullion, you'll get the most for your money by buying either Austrian Coronas or South African Krugerrands. These generally sell for 1 percent over the spot price, whereas other, more popular gold coins may sell at a premium of 5 percent or more. Surprisingly, Coronas and Krugerrands are usually a better deal than gold bars.

$CROOGE INVESTING TIP #83

Buy 1-Ounce Gold Coins, Not Fractional Ones
Gold bullion coins are minted in sizes ranging from 1/10 ounce to more than 1 ounce. You'll get significantly more gold for your money if you buy the 1-ounce coins instead of the fractional coins. Two 1/2-ounce gold coins generally cost 3.5 to 5 percent more than a 1-ounce gold coin. Four 1/4-ounce gold coins are generally 6 to 9 percent more expensive than a 1-ounce coin. Ten 1/10-ounce gold coins are 10 to 22 percent more expensive than the 1-ounce coins.

$CROOGE INVESTING TIP #84

Look for Bargains in Semirare and Rare Coins
Rare coins go through cycles, like any other investment. For example, common-dated Morgan silver dollars in mint (MS65) condition jumped from $100 each in the early 1980s to $850 in 1986. Today, you can pick them up for $100

again! Start bargain hunting today. It pays to shop around for top-quality rare coins, but one place to start is Van Simmons, David Hall's North American Trading Group (1936 E. Deere, Suite 102, Santa Ana, CA 92705; 800-359-4255). He has years of experience in gold and silver rare coins at the best prices. (Also check out David Hall's auction Web site, www.collectorsuniverse.com.)

Collecting old silver dollars (Morgan and Peace dollars) has a lot of practical value, too. A friend of mine has a very successful method of rewarding his employees and encouraging them to work harder: When they do outstanding work, he gives them a shiny U.S. silver dollar. Employees love getting them because they seem more valuable than a cash bonus. His silver dollar bonus plan makes his employees feel happy and work harder.

He also says that most employees assume such silver dollars are worth $15 to $20 each. Scrooge Investors and business people like this idea: giving bonuses that employees think are worth a lot more than they are! The coins cost under $10 each in circulated condition today. I'm not talking about worn out coins. These are good-quality coins in very fine (VF) condition or better.

Silver dollars are a Scrooge bargain, either as an investment or as an incentive program in your business. I know travelers who give them away as special tips. Instead of slipping a few bucks to the bellhop or airport skycap, hand them a shiny silver dollar minted a hundred years ago and watch the strange but happy look on their faces. It's also a great way to introduce Americans to their monetary roots . . . when a dollar was worth its weight in silver! There's something special about holding an old silver dollar in your hand.

To purchase silver dollars, check any of the coin dealers mentioned above. One of the lowest-priced coin dealers specializing in silver dollars is Bert Blumert, President of Camino Coins (P.O. Box 4292, Burlingame, CA 94011; 800-348-8001). He's the grand old man of silver.

$CROOGE INVESTING TIP #85

Take Delivery in States With No Sales Tax on Coins and Bullion
Sales tax on coins and bullion varies from state to state, from zero to 10 percent, including local and county taxes. You can usually escape the tax entirely by purchasing coins from out of state, although there have been increasing efforts by state tax authorities to force mail-order firms to charge individual state sales taxes (see Table 11-1). Already, major brokerage houses will charge you state sales tax if you take delivery of coin purchases. However, coin purchases are exempt from tax if you let the broker hold the coins for you.

Generally, I don't recommend buying coins from brokerage houses because you lose privacy; they demand your Social Security number even when you buy (it's required by law only when you sell). And they won't take cash.

If you want maximum privacy and the lowest cost per coin, I recommend shopping locally in a state that exempts coins from the sales tax. Surprisingly, about half of all states now exempt all or almost all coin sales, and the list is growing. Exemption is becoming popular because these states know that they are losing business to mail-order firms in other states that do not charge sales tax. For the private Scrooge Investor, buying gold and silver in person at a local coin dealer is the best way to go. Just walk into the coin shop, select your investment, pay with cash, and walk out the door. No name or Social Security number is recorded. However, I recommend that you get a receipt for tax purposes in case you sell later.

$CROOGE INVESTING TIP #86

Be Aware of the Cheapest Way to Buy Precious Metals
The cheapest way to buy precious metals is to go to a commodities broker, buy a futures contract for the nearest delivery date, and take delivery. For a nominal fee, your precious metals will be stored in a safe, secure, exchange-approved warehouse. Just remember, the minimum purchases are high. Table 11-2 lists the minimums, depending on the exchange.

TABLE 11-1   State Sales Tax Reference Guide

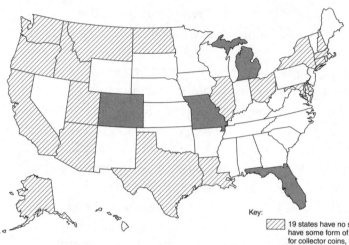

Key:

19 states have no state sales use tax at all or have some form of state sales/use tax exemption for collector coins, bullion coins, and/or other forms of bullion.

4 states have bills introduced or efforts underway to secure a sales/use tax exemption for collector coins, bullion coins, and/or other forms of bullion.

State	State Tax Rate[1]	(as of October 9, 1997) Collector Coins	Bullion Coins	Bullion
Alabama	4%	taxed	taxed	taxed
Alaska	No state sales tax			
Arizona	5%	exempt	exempt	exempt[2]
Arkansas	4.5%	taxed	taxed	taxed
California	6%	exempt[3]	exempt[3]	exempt[3]
Colorado	3%	taxed	taxed	taxed
Connecticut	6%	exempt[4]	exempt[3]	exempt[3]
Delaware	No state sales tax			
District of Columbia	5.75%	taxed	taxed	taxed
Florida	6%[4]	taxed	taxed	taxed
Georgia	4%	taxed	taxed	taxed
Hawaii	4%	taxed	taxed	taxed
Idaho	5%	exempt[2]	exempt[2]	exempt[2]

(Continued)

TABLE 11-1   State Sales Tax Reference Guide *(Continued)*

State	State Tax Rate[1]	Collector Coins	Bullion Coins	Bullion
Illinois	6.25%	exempt	exempt	exempt
Indiana	5%	taxed	taxed	taxed
Iowa	5%	taxed	taxed	taxed
Kansas	4.9%	taxed	taxed	taxed
Kentucky	6%	taxed	taxed	taxed
Louisiana	4%	exempt[3]	exempt[3]	taxed
Maine	6%	taxed	taxed	taxed
Maryland[5]	5%	exempt[3]	exempt[3]	exempt[3]
Massachusetts	5%	exempt[3]	exempt[3]	exempt[3]
Michigan	6%	taxed	taxed	taxed
Minnesota	6.5%	taxed	taxed	taxed
Mississippi	7%	taxed	taxed	taxed
Missouri	4.225%	taxed	taxed	taxed
Montana	No state sales tax			
Nebraska	5%	taxed	taxed	taxed
Nevada	6.5%	taxed	taxed	taxed
New Hampshire	No state sales tax			
New Jersey	6%	taxed	taxed	taxed
New Mexico	5%	taxed	taxed	taxed
New York[5]	4%	taxed	exempt[3]	exempt[3]
North Carolina	4%	taxed	taxed	taxed
North Dakota	5%	exempt	exempt	taxed
Ohio	5%	exempt	exempt	exempt
Oklahoma	4.5%	taxed	taxed	taxed
Oregon	No state sales tax			
Pennsylvania	6%	taxed	taxed	taxed
Rhode Island	7%	exempt	exempt	exempt
South Carolina	5%	taxed	taxed	taxed

(Continued)

TABLE 11-1   State Sales Tax Reference Guide *(Continued)*

State	State Tax Rate[1]	Collector Coins	Bullion Coins	Bullion
South Dakota	4%	taxed	taxed	taxed
Tennessee	6%	taxed	taxed	taxed
Texas	6.25%	exempt[3]	exempt[3]	exempt[3]
Utah	4.875%	exempt	exempt	exempt
Vermont	5%	taxed	taxed	taxed
Virginia	3.5%	taxed	taxed	taxed
Washington	6.5%	exempt	exempt	exempt
West Virginia	6%	taxed	taxed	taxed
Wisconsin	5%	taxed	taxed	taxed
Wyoming	4%	taxed	taxed	taxed

1 Figures for the state tax rate do not include any local taxes. Source: Compiled by the Tax Foundation from a survey of state revenue officers.

2 Bullion for use in jewelry and works of art is not exempt.

3 Exemption applies only to sales of $1000 or more.

4 Exemption becomes effective July 1, 1996.

5 To be considered a wholesale transaction, dealers must have a special license in these states. A home state resale certificate will not be recognized by these states. Other states may have this provision as well, but only Maryland and New York have come to ICTA's attention.

NOTE: Under certain circumstances, delivery of merchandise to an out-of-state destination may release the dealer (vendor) from a sales/use tax collection obligation. However, depending on the sales/use tax laws in the destination state, the recipient (customer) may be liable for the payment of use tax. There have been instances where the customer has received a demand from the state taxing authority for payment of the use tax plus interest and penalties.

SOURCE: Industry Council for Tangible Assets, P.O. Box 1365, Severna Park, MD 21146-8365; 410-626-7005; fax: 410-626-7007. The information contained herein is for information purposes only and has been compiled from sources deemed reliable. However, changes in sales tax rates and exemptions may occur without notice, and you should not rely solely on this data. ICTA cannot be held responsible for any errors, either typographical or in fact.

$CROOGE INVESTING TIP #87

The Best Way to Invest in Platinum Is Low-Premium Bullion Coins

During much of the 1990s, the platinum group metals were far more exciting than silver and gold, with palladium (platinum's sister metal) reaching an all-time high, even going above the price of platinum for the first time in history. Plat-

TABLE 11-2 Precious Metals Purchases

Metal	Exchange	Minimum Purchase
Gold	Chicago Board of Trade	1 kilo (32.15 troy oz.)
Gold	MidAmerica Exchange	1 kilo
Gold	COMEX	100 troy oz.
Silver	Chicago Board of Trade	1000 troy oz.
Silver	COMEX	5000 troy oz.
Silver	MidAmerica Exchange	1000 troy oz.
Platinum	MidAmerica Exchange	25 troy oz.
Platinum	New York Mercantile	50 troy oz.
Palladium	New York Mercantile	100 troy oz.

inum itself soared above the price of gold, even though historically it has traded below gold. In 1999, platinum hit $400 an ounce, whereas gold stayed under $300.

Since most of the world's platinum is produced in Russia, tight supplies in platinum occasionally develop, largely from bureaucratic snafus. On the demand side, there's been a boom in the demand for platinum for use in jewelry and coinage (see Table 11-3). In 1997, the United States began issuing an eagle bullion coin that has proved to be popular among investors. Buy through the brokers listed above.

Unfortunately, platinum bullion is nowhere near as liquid as gold and silver bullion. That means investors in platinum and palladium bullion may have to sell at a price lower than

TABLE 11-3 Popular Platinum Coins

Coin	Denomination	Issue Date
American Eagle	1, ½, ¼, ⅒ oz.	1997–present
Australian Koala	1, ½, ¼, ⅒, ⅟₂₀ oz.	1988–present
Australian Koala large bullion coins	1 kilo, 10 oz., 2 oz.	1993–present
Canadian Maple Leaf	1, ½, ¼, ⅒, ⅟₂₀ oz.	1988–present
Isle of Man Noble	1, ½, ¼, ⅒ oz.	1983–present

the spot price. However, the liquidity of the market has been helped in recent years by the advent of low-premium platinum bullion coins, which are targeted at investors. Following are some of the more popular platinum coins and the denominations available. As with gold bullion coins, the lower the denomination you buy, the higher the premium you'll pay.

$CROOGE INVESTING TIP #88

Go to These Web Sites for Free Data on Gold, Silver, and Platinum

The following Web sites offer free market data on gold, silver, and platinum. All of them are sponsored by the precious metals industry, so they all have a bullish bias. Nevertheless, they all offer solid, reliable, statistical data and news related to these markets.

Gold-Eagle is a free site with news, reports, commentary, and analysis of the gold markets from a variety of sources. Go to www.gold-eagle.com.

Gold Field Mineral Services has been a source of reliable information on the worldwide gold market for years. Based in London, a lot of its publications, such as the *Annual Gold Survey, The World Silver Survey,* and *Precious Metals Quarterly,* are for sale (and probably are too expensive for the individual Scrooge Investor). But you will find some free information on the site as well as links to related sites. Go to www.gfms.co.uk/html.

The Silver Institute is a useful site for silver investors. It's updated frequently, so it's a good site to bookmark. Go to www.silverinstitute.org.

The Platinum Guild International has one of the better sites for precious metals investors. It has online reports, videos, virtual radio market news, charts— almost anything the diligent Scrooge Investor needs when considering an investment in platinum. It also offers a free daily e-mail newsletter that covers news and market action related to gold and silver as well as platinum. Go to www.platinumguild.org.

$CROOGE INVESTING TIP #89

For Junior Mining Stocks, Go to Brokers Who Make a Specialty of It

The Scrooge Investor can double, triple, or even quadruple his money in short order by investing in junior mining stocks during a bull market in commodities. It is the preferred way to leverage profits during an inflationary boom.

But you have to be wary, because junior exploration and developmental mining companies are treacherous. You can make 100 percent on your money in a day, but you can also lose your shirt in short order.

If you are going to get involved in this high-risk sector, I suggest you work through a brokerage firm that specializes in junior mining shares. Here is a list of my favorites, all of which have been in business for many years.

- Rick Rule, Global Resource Investments, La Jolla, CA; 800-477-7853 or 760-943-3939; fax 760-943-3938.

- Kevin Smith, National Resource Group, Seattle, WA; 800-426-9494 or 206-622-7200; fax 206-343-6116.

- Woody Littlefield, Century Capital Corp., Columbia, SC; 800-752-3233 or 864-233-2131; fax 760-233-2178.

12

SAVING MONEY WHEN YOU BUY AND SELL REAL ESTATE

You may buy land now as cheap as stinking mackerel.

—William Shakespeare

REAL ESTATE INVESTING HAS ALWAYS been one of the premier ways to become financially independent. Moreover, stock investors have always been attracted to real estate as a way to diversify out of stocks.

Yet real estate is also the most expensive investment to buy, sell, and lease, due to closing costs, commissions, and other expenses. Fortunately, you can cut your costs tremendously when you buy real estate. At every stage, from finding the property to closing the deal, there are opportunities to save money. Scratch beneath the surface of any successful real estate investor and you'll find a real Scrooge.

$CROOGE INVESTING TIP #90

Heed Some Advice From John Schaub on Buying Right

One of my favorite real estate experts is John Schaub, a man who truly knows how to be a skinflint. He has survived and prospered in the booms and busts in real estate over the last 30 years because he is so careful in risk management. He buys only 1 out of every 100 homes or properties he examines. Here are some of his tips on buying right:

- *Before you start, make a list of exactly what you want in a property.*

- *Become well-versed in the market by systematically examining properties, talking to sellers, and making offers.* You might also hire appraisers. They're usually well worth the $100 or so they charge.

- *Deal directly with the owner rather than an agent or employee.* The owner knows better than anyone what the bottom price will be. If you're looking at newspaper ads, concentrate on the "For Sale By Owner" ads.

- *Find someone who is anxious to sell.* You might read obituaries to find the representative of an estate to see whether the deceased's house will be sold. Loan companies might tell you about people who are behind on their loans. Check public records to see who has filed for divorce. As you drive through prospective neighborhoods, look for houses that look as though no one lives in them. Work with out-of-state banks that own local properties they need to sell.

- *Before you make an offer, always find out from the public record what sellers paid for the property and how long they owned it.*

- *Always make an offer.* Even if it's refused, you learn something about how people react. The more offers you make, the better you'll be at it.

- *When you meet better negotiators, study their techniques, but don't try to outsmart them.*

- *Remember the 10-10-10 guidelines.* Buy at a price at least 10 percent below the market value. Pay a maximum interest rate of 10 percent (easy to do with today's low interest rates). Negotiate hard on interest and drive it as low as possible. Make a maximum down payment of 10 percent.

Schaub and other real estate experts also recommend that you take full advantage of distress sales, which appear to be a growth industry in the 1990s—foreclosures are big business. Be on the lookout for superbargains—sometimes 30 percent or more below the appraised market—from banks, the IRS, or the Department of Veterans Affairs (VA). During the 1990s, the Resolution Trust Corporation (RTC), set up by Congress to bail out the savings and loan industry, offered thousands of properties at bargain prices, and hundreds of Scrooge real estate investors, including John Schaub, made out like bandits.

If you're planning to buy real estate, I strongly urge you to get a copy of Schaub's book, *Buying Right,* and to subscribe to his newsletter. You can order the book from Pro Serve, 1938 Ringling Blvd., Sarasota, FL 34236; 800-237-9222 (includes Canada) or 727-366-9024; price: $16.95, including postage. Also check out his Web site: www.makingitbig.org.

John also publishes an excellent real estate newsletter, *John Schaub's Strategies and Solutions.* Subscriptions are $47.00 a year for six issues. Mention this book and he'll send you a free sample copy.

If you're really interested in Schaub's successful approach to buying single-family homes, get a copy of his most popular tape series, *Making It Big on Little Deals,* available for only $149, including postage. It's well worth the price, and it's up-to-date advice.

$CROOGE INVESTING TIP #91

Find a Top-Notch Appraiser

Whether you're buying or selling real estate, a top-notch appraiser can help you to find out what a house is worth. You'll probably pay a hundred dollars or more for an appraisal. An appraisal will also help you to get a loan, because most banks won't give you a loan unless you're buying a property for what it's worth.

You can get the names of appraisers from your real estate agent or your banker. You can also check out many appraisers' qualifications—or get the names of qualified appraisers in your area—by going online. Go to www.asc.gov. This is the Web site of the Appraisal Subcommittee of the Federal Financial Institutions Examination Council.

It will tell you just about everything you need to know about appraisers and give you a list of registered appraisers in your state. It will also give you an automatic e-mail notice about any disciplinary actions against a particular appraiser, such as license revocations or suspensions. Not every real estate appraiser will be listed on this site, but many will be.

$CROOGE INVESTING TIP #92

Shop for the Best Mortgage

When you're looking for a mortgage, it pays to call several lenders and compare rates. Don't just go with your broker's recommendation. Figure out how much you will pay each month for each scenario. For adjustable-rate mortgages (ARMs), assume that interest rates will rise to the maximum allowed by law. Read all mortgage documents carefully. Make sure that they don't contain a lot of restrictive clauses or add-on charges. Some may require that you pay the bank's attorney fees and processing expenses. Negotiate to have these removed.

One useful resource is the *Home Buyers Mortgage Kit.* Included in the kit is a listing of the mortgage rates and terms available in 36 major metropolitan areas around the country.

It's an easy way to compare rates among various mortgage lenders. Also included is *How To Shop for Your Mortgage,* a 56-page booklet designed to educate homeowners about the mortgage market. The kit costs $20, plus $3 postage and handling. For information or to order, contact HSH Associates, 1200 Route 23 North, Butler, NJ 07405; 800-UPDATES; 973-838-3330; www.hsh.com.

$CROOGE INVESTING TIP #93

Beware of Hidden Fees If You Shop for a Mortgage Online

Whether you're planning to refinance your existing home or buy a new home, it's important to watch mortgage rates closely. Online services have made shopping for a mortgage loan easier than ever. You don't have to traipse around from bank to bank getting rate quotes. You can get them and compare them online at the touch of a button.

Unfortunately, there are some pitfalls and some unscrupulous lenders online who will cheat you. How do you protect yourself and make sure you get the lowest rate?

First, make sure the Web site lists the annual percentage rate you'll pay, also called the APR. The APR shows the true cost of the loan, including points and loan origination fees. Steer clear of Web sites that don't show the APR.

Second, find out how the Web site operator is being paid. Is it acting as a direct lender, a mortgage broker, or a referral service? If it's a mortgage broker, is it getting a flat fee from borrowers to find the best loan? Or is it getting a bonus, sometimes known as a "yield-spread premium," a "back-end fee," or an "overage." Such kickbacks or sweetheart deals can add 1 percent to the cost of your loan. Avoid them.

Third, does the Web site provide your personal information to others? Avoid those that do. You're giving a lot of sensitive financial information to a mortgage lender, and you don't want to have that information sold, rented, or traded to another company.

Fourth, make sure the lender is licensed in your state. Check with the Better Business Bureau as well. You don't want to be dealing with a sleazy operator.

There are a mind-boggling 3000 mortgage lenders online, so you have plenty of sites to choose from. The following Web sites are good places to start your search for an online mortgage.

- *HomeShark* (www.rateshop.homeshark.com/scripts/ crateship.dll) is one of the Web's leading mortgage sites. Simply click on your state to get quick reports and current rates from several lenders in your area.

- *I-own* (www.iown.com) will give you a list of 10 lenders ranked by important factors like closing costs, interest rate, or monthly payment. I-own charges a half-point fee to process the loan.

- *HSH Associates* (www.hsh.com) is a great source of objective data, because it doesn't make loans or accept lender advertising. What it does do is survey some 2500 mortgage lenders and update its rates daily.

$CROOGE INVESTING TIP #94

Save Big Money on Closing Costs and Commissions

The best way to save on closing costs is to avoid dealing with banks and mortgage companies altogether. Use Schaub's technique of financing directly with sellers. You'll avoid all the costs associated with a bank loan, such as a second appraisal and mortgage title insurance. If you're an experienced investor, you can also save money by not having properties appraised.

Here's a little-known way to eliminate the 6 percent sales commission and reduce closing costs when selling a house: Lease your property with an option to buy!

Here's how a lease option works: Suppose you want to sell a rental house appraised for $115,000. Place a classified ad in the local paper that reads, "Rent with option to buy."

You offer to rent the place for $900 a month, higher than the market rent. The rental income consists of $700 rent and a $200 option fee. The option permits the tenants to buy the property for $115,000 at any time during the ensuing year. Set a price that tenants will find attractive. It has to be a good deal for both parties or a lease option won't work.

Here are the benefits of a lease option:

- You get an additional $200 a month in income, part or all of which you get to keep if the tenant does not exercise the option.

- Option fees are not taxable to you until the option is exercised or abandoned.

- You avoid the 6 percent real estate agent's commission when you sell the house. This is a potential savings of $7000 in our example.

- Even if the option is not exercised, your property is likely to be better maintained. Renters with a lease option take better care of their future home.

Schaub publishes a special report on lease options, called *Lease Options,* which contains sample contracts and all the details. To obtain a copy, send $19 to Pro Serve, 1938 Ringling Blvd., Sarasota, FL 34236; 800-237-9222 (including Canada) or 727-366-9024.

$CROOGE INVESTING TIP #95

Buy a No-Load Fund in Real Estate

Do you want to invest in real estate but not hunt for properties, negotiate deals, and perform the countless other necessary tasks? Check out Columbia Real Estate Equity (800-547-1707). It had a total return of 12.33 percent in 1998. Also, it's no-load, and the minimum investment is $1000. According to Reuters News Service, it has been 30 percent less volatile than its typical peer during the last three years.

$CROOGE INVESTING TIP #96

Buy Mortgages at a Discount and Earn 15 Percent or More

One great income-producing investment is the discounted mortgage market, which offers several advantages over real estate: better liquidity, better cash flow, no management responsibilities, and rates of return exceeding 20 percent if you shop carefully.

On the downside, you receive no tax breaks and you can't profit from the property's appreciation unless the owner defaults. Default is a danger; you may end up with a piece of property that has little value.

Here's how discounted mortgages work: Many sellers of real estate have taken back second mortgages to close the deal. Many holders of second mortgages would like to sell them before they mature because they need the money sooner. They have income tax problems or they fear they won't get paid, especially if balloon payments are involved.

For these and other reasons, many such holders will sell their seconds at a substantial discount. For example, a $10,000, five-year note at 12 percent interest means that the seller is getting $222 a month. Suppose four years are left on the second and the seller wants out. The balance due after one year is $8450. If you purchased the second for $7800, which sounds like a reasonable offer, you would earn 20 percent on your money.

Where do you find second mortgages?

- Contact several real estate brokers in your area and let them know you are willing to buy seconds.

- Go to your local county deed office and get the names of individuals who have seconds on properties.

- Place classified ads in the local newspaper saying, "Private party has cash to buy existing notes and mortgages."

The following are some important caveats:

- Before buying seconds, check the financial condition of the property owners, especially their main sources of income.

- Stay away from mortgages with large balloon payments, which are seldom paid off on time and must be renegotiated.

- Make sure lots of equity is in the property.

- If the owner defaults on your second, he or she may default on the first mortgage as well. To collect your money, you must continue paying the first mortgage while you foreclose on the house! Otherwise, you'll likely end up with nothing.

- Avoid leveraging debt; don't borrow money from a bank or credit card to buy a note.

- Don't tell the owner of the property that you are buying the note at a discount. He or she may want to pay it off to save money.

- Finally, beware of such closing costs as title insurance and recording the second at the courthouse. Closing costs can reduce your real return significantly.

Obviously, this introduction to discount mortgage investing only scratches the surface. Real estate expert Schaub has an excellent six-hour tape series called *Investing in Paper*. It covers investing in first and second mortgages and includes a 65-page workbook. You can order the tapes from Pro Serve for $149, including postage. (See address above.) You will also get a free copy of Jim Napier's book, *Invest in Debt: The "How To" Book on Buying Paper for Cash Flow*. Separately, it's $12.

13

SAVING A BUNDLE ON RARE COINS, COLLECTIBLES, AND ANTIQUES

Beware of little expenses. A small leak will sink a great ship.

—Ben Franklin

ART AND COLLECTIBLES ARE ANOTHER area into which stock investors seek to diversify. Yet nowhere is there more overcharging than in collectibles. Why? Because most buyers don't know value. Dealers can charge high markups mainly because the customers willingly pay them without doing their homework.

Indeed, it's not unusual for markups to range from 15 percent to 50 percent, and sometimes even higher. If you're buying from a dealer in the collectibles market, you're almost always buying at the full retail price. Moreover, when you sell to a dealer, you're almost always selling at the wholesale price, maybe even below it if you're dealing with a shrewd dealer. A Scrooge Investor should strive to do the opposite: Buy below wholesale; sell at retail!

$CROOGE INVESTING TIP #97

Buy What You Love!

Perhaps the best advice in buying collectibles is to buy what you love. Whether it's baseball cards, rare coins, or old Uncle Scrooge comic books, buy it because you enjoy it. If you buy simply to make money, you may end up chasing the latest fad.

If you're passionate about a subject, you'll become an expert in it. You'll be eager to read everything you can about it, chart the prices in auction catalogs, and learn about subtle variations that less knowledgeable investors will miss. You'll develop a trained eye. You'll become an expert. You'll be able to find the bargains. You'll be able to enjoy the object for its aesthetic and historic value, so even if you don't make a killing on your collectible, you still get your money's worth.

$CROOGE INVESTING TIP #98

Learn to Evaluate the Condition of the Collectibles

As one collectibles expert says, "Just as in real estate, the magic word is location, location, location, so in collectibles, it is condition, condition, condition. Collectors in some fields are absolute fanatics about condition."

"For instance," he adds, "comic book people are amazingly stringent in their requirements. If that staple has a tiny bit of rust on it, that can downgrade your book. Sheet music people are the same way. They don't want a cat hair, they don't want a tear, they don't want your name written in the upper corner."

The best way to learn value is to attend auctions, visit shops, ask questions of the experts and read everything you can find about the collectibles you're interested in. The public library is a great place to start. For information on

10,000 resources for 2600 categories of collectibles, consult *Maloney's Antiques & Collectibles Resource Directory* (Collector's Information Clearinghouse, P.O. Box 2049, Frederick, MD 21702-1049; 301-695-8544 or 800-836-2403; www.maloneysonline.com).

$CROOGE INVESTING TIP #99

Know the Value of the Collectibles You're Buying
You need to know not only how to evaluate the condition of an item but also what price to pay for it. An almost microscopic scratch on a rare coin, for example, could cut the value by more than half. A particular carnival glass vase could sell for anywhere from $30 to $800, depending on its color. That's how finicky some collectors are.

Again, you can learn something about value by shopping around and asking questions. Some excellent price guides are also available. One good general price guide is the *Collector Magazine and Price Guide* (P.O. Box 1050, Dubuque, IA 52004; 800-334-7165 or 319-588-2073; $19.95 per year, $3.50 per copy). The company also offers publications geared to specific areas of collecting—*Post Card Collector, The Military Trader, The Toy Trader, Discoveries* (about music), and *The Big Reel* (about movies). To find out more about each publication, go to its Web site: www.collect.com.

Each specialty, if large enough, may have its own price guides. In rare coins, for example, the best guides are the *Coin Dealer Newsletter* for wholesale raw coins and the *Certified Coin Dealer Newsletter* for coins that have been graded through a grading service such as Professional Coin Grading Service, Numismatic Guarantee Corp., Numismatic Certification Institute, or American Numismatic Association Certification Service (P.O. Box 11099, Torrance, CA 90504; www.greysheet.com). Published weekly, these newsletters give the recent wholesale prices of the most widely traded U.S. rare coins. Subscription prices for the *Coin Dealer*

Newsletter are $54 for six months, $98 for one year, and $162 for two years. For CCDN, it's $65 for six months, $117 for one year, and $193 for two years. Their *Currency Dealer Newsletter,* which covers paper money, is available for $23 for six months or $44 for a year.

$CROOGE INVESTING TIP #100

Comparison Shop Between Galleries and Dealers
It's hard to shop for collectibles because each one is different. It's like comparing apples and kumquats in many cases. That's where expertise comes in handy.

Another problem is finding dealers who handle the items you're interested in. If you collect alpaca sweaters, you might find that the dealers for such an esoteric item are spread far and wide. With more common items, such as U.S. coins or stamps, comparison shopping is considerably easier, although no two coins or stamps are exactly alike either. An excellent sourcebook, which cross-indexes dealers and collectors according to their specialties, is *Trash or Treasure* (updated every six months). It's a good place to find all the major buyers in a particular item. The book is available from Treasure Hunt Publications, P.O. Box 3028, Pismo Beach, CA 93448; 805-773-6777 or 800-479-6836 for orders only. The price is $34 postpaid.

Tony Hyman, President of Treasure Hunt Publications, stresses the importance of knowing where to go when buying or selling specialty items. For example, a man picked up a Parker Astec gold pen for only $55 at a garage sale and turned around and sold it to a specialty dealer (listed in *I'll Buy That Too!*) for $15,000! There are two lessons here for the Scrooge Investor: (1) If you're selling a unique item, make sure you're getting full value (in the above example, the homeowner in charge of the garage sale got taken); and (2) it pays to shop garage and estate sales for bargains and then sell your finds to the right collectors.

$CROOGE INVESTING TIP #101

Buy Fine Art at 50 Percent Off Retail

Here's a little-known way to get 25 to 50 percent off the retail price of any artwork or collectible you see in a gallery: Use my recommended discount art broker, Fine Arts Ltd. My subscribers and I have been using Fine Arts for years and have saved thousands on beautiful paintings, sculptures, prints, rare books, and other artwork. I've never received so many rave letters from Scrooge Investors about a money-saving service.

Suppose you see a piece of artwork you like in a gallery, but the price is too high. Call Michael Kuschmann, President of Fine Arts Ltd., and he will contact his contacts around the country to see if he can obtain the same artwork at wholesale. He may even go directly to the gallery where you saw the piece and get a wholesale bid. Once he obtains the artwork, he charges his price plus a 10 percent markup. Believe me, that's an incredible savings.

Let me give you some real-life examples of subscribers who saved thousands of dollars using this discount art dealer.

- One subscriber was just about to purchase an Erte bronze statue for full retail: $16,000. The salesperson refused to budge on the price for this beautiful bronze piece. My subscriber walked out of the store, called Fine Arts Ltd., and got the statue for $9750. Total savings: $7570 or 47 percent of the retail price.

- Recently, in Las Vegas, I saw a beautiful color print called Mozart in the Forum gallery. The gallery wanted $2250, plus $1200 for a frame—an outrageous price. I called Fine Arts Ltd. and got it for $1500 framed, saving more than 50 percent off the retail price.

- Another subscriber saw a large Jiang bronze in a gallery. He admired the sculpture, but the price tag was a steep $32,000. The gallery wasn't willing to negotiate. He called Kuschmann, who contacted his sources around the country. One of his agents had a good relationship with the same gallery and negotiated a wholesale price for the same Jiang bronze. Kuschmann informed the buyer that his price was $16,000 delivered, half the gallery price. My subscriber quickly agreed to the price, and Kuschmann put a hold on the item. A few days later another couple visited the gallery and were willing to buy the Jiang at full retail, $32,000! Needless to say, the gallery was distraught. This sculpture had been on display for a year and a half, so they were willing to unload it at a discount to Kuschmann. Suddenly, there were two bids on it. The gallery was hurting from the recession and sorely wanted to sell the bronze at full price, but they had an obligation to honor the first offer. The gallery told Kuschmann that unless full payment was received in 24 hours, the deal was off. Kuschmann had to scramble to get the funds sent overnight from the buyer. Fortunately, the money was sent in time, and the Jiang bronze is now proudly displayed in the subscriber's living room.

Fine Arts Ltd. can't save 50 percent every time, but it can cut 25 percent or more off the prices of most art and collectibles.

I recommend that you contact Fine Arts Ltd. before you make any major purchase at a gallery, show, or even on the Internet. For more information on saving money on art, contact Michael B. Kuschmann, President, Fine Arts Ltd., 172 W. Comstock Ave., Suite 203, Winter Park, FL 32789; 800-229-4322 or 407-702-6638; fax 407-629-6709.

Kuschmann, by the way, specializes in limited prints at a discount. Limited prints, often signed by the artist, have become an affordable way to profit from the art explosion. Original paintings and drawings from famous artists can sell for millions. Only the superrich can afford to buy them. Limited-edition signed prints are a viable alternative for private investors who want to create a nice collection. A few hundred lithographs, etchings, or silk screen prints are made, and then the plates are destroyed. The artist signs the prints, which are then sold to the public. Limited-edition signed prints have also skyrocketed in price, but you don't have to pay retail. You can save about 30 percent by avoiding the high-priced galleries in resorts and major cities and purchasing your prints by mail. Fine Arts Ltd. can handle everything for you, no matter where you live. The company has been in business since 1976. Kuschmann includes works by Renoir, Picasso, Erte, Rembrandt, Chagall, Delacroix, and McKnight. Several years ago, I wanted to buy a McKnight print. Most of the galleries wanted about $1400 for the print I was looking for. Fine Arts Ltd. sold it to me for $950.

$CROOGE INVESTING TIP #102

Avoid Chasing Fads

Fads come and go in collectibles. When Mark McGwire was on his home run chase, Mark McGwire collectibles— old baseball cards, autographs, and other items—soared sky-high. Afterward, they fell back to more reasonable levels.

This is especially true for toys. Remember Cabbage Patch dolls, Elmos, and Furbies. Now, Beanie Babies are the craze. They're selling for anywhere from $5 into the thousands. By the time you read this book, another mania undoubtedly will have replaced them. Just as you don't want to buy at retail and sell at wholesale, you also don't want to buy when an item is hot and sell when it's not.

$CROOGE INVESTING TIP #103

Buy Through Auctions

Auctions can be a wonderful place to buy collectibles. Sometimes you can buy at auction cheaper than you can anywhere else. Many dealers do much of their buying at auctions. Here are a few tips:

- Attend specialized auctions of particular items rather than large, general auctions at which a wide variety of items are sold. You could spend a lot of time at a general auction before you find what you're looking for, and you will probably have to pay more.

- Attend wholesale auctions, which have large numbers of dealers.

- Attend auctions at which there is a need to sell, such as estate sales, bankruptcies, and IRS auctions.

- Attend auctions at which there is no minimum bid.

- Set price limits on each item you're bidding on, and don't go beyond your dollar limit.

Auctions are usually advertised in the weekend section of major newspapers. You can also get on mailing lists for auctions in your area by calling up the auctioneers in the yellow pages and asking them to keep you informed of upcoming events.

The country's two leading auction houses are Sotheby's (1334 York Ave., New York, NY 10021; 800-444-3709 or 212-606-7000) and Christie's Fine Art Auctioneers (20 Rockefeller Plaza, New York, NY 10020; 800-395 6300 or 212-636-2000). Each offers dozens of catalogs every year. Subscriptions run from $15 to $800 a year, but if you're a serious auction buyer, they can be well worth it. Write or call both companies for a brochure describing their publications.

$CROOGE INVESTING TIP #104

Buy and Sell at Internet Auctions

The Internet has revolutionized the auction business. When Mark McGwire's record-setting 70th home run ball was auctioned, it was done over the Internet. You can buy everything from Pez dispensers to collectible cars online. However, you're better off sticking with items below about $5000 when buying over the Internet.

If you sell at online auctions, you'll pay lower commissions. At live auctions, the commissions are usually 15 percent on items under $50,000. The industry standard for online auction houses is under 5 percent.

The number of online auction houses is mind-boggling—more than 1000. One Web site, Auction Watch (www.auctionwatch.com), monitors more than 300 of them. If you're a beginner, you're probably better off sticking with the major sites, like eBay (www.ebay.com), Christie's (www.christies.com), and Sotheby's (www.Sothebys.Amazon. com).

Another top-of-the-line online auction site for top-quality collectibles is www. collectorsuniverse.com.

Here's how they usually work. You register with the site, surf it until something strikes your fancy, and then bid on it. An online auction can last from a few hours to a few days. If you're the winning bidder, then you negotiate payment and delivery terms with the seller.

Other useful Web sites include Buy Collectibles (www.buycollectibles.com), which has a searchable database for items; Collector Online (www.collectoronline.com), which matches buyers and sellers; and Interactive Collector (www.icollector.com), which has catalogs from international dealers on its Web site.

$CROOGE INVESTING TIP #105

Avoid the Pitfalls of Online Auctions

Unfortunately, online auctions have become hotbeds of fraud. Sellers sometimes fail to deliver, or they don't deliver what they've promised. You can get stuck with a fake or a reproduction. According to the Internet Fraud Watch, sponsored by the National Consumers League in Washington, D.C., auction fraud was the top online complaint in 1998. However, it's estimated that less than 1 percent of transactions are fraudulent, so your chances of getting taken are slim. By taking a few simple steps to protect yourself, you'll reduce that to almost nothing.

- *Know the seller.* Deal with a site that requires online sellers to register. eBay, for example, requires a seller's social security number and other personal information. The seller's identity is then confirmed through Equifax, a major credit bureau. Some online auction firms have chat rooms or feedback forums devoted to complaints against certain sellers. Read these and find out if a seller has received lots of complaints.

    eBay also protects sellers. For example, they won't let you register using a free and anonymous e-mail account, such as Hotmail, unless you're also willing to give them your credit card number.

- *If you're selling online, make it clear that you won't ship until you receive a check from the buyer and the check clears.*

- *Use an escrow service for purchases of over $200.* An online escrow service acts as an intermediary between you and the seller. You pay a fee (usually 2 to 10 percent of the sale price, with a minimum of about $5). The escrow service holds on to the funds until you've received the merchandise and inspected it. When you accept the item, your funds are released to the seller. If you return the item, then the funds are released back to you. Among the online escrow services are Auction Universe (www.auctionuniverse.com); i-Escrow (www. iescrow.com); and Tradesafe (www.tradesafe.com).

- *Insure purchases of $200 or less.* Some online auctions offer insurance. If your purchase turns out to be misrepresented, you can file a claim and be reimbursed. eBay, for example, provides up to $200 worth of coverage through Lloyd's of London. Under Auction Universe's Bidsafe Gold program, you can get an insurance policy that covers up to $3000 in damage during shipping. The cost is $19.95 a year.

- *Pay by credit card.* You can withhold your payment if you don't get what you've been promised. This works if the seller is an auction house or a dealer. But if the seller is an individual, then it's more difficult. For a fee of $19.95, Auction Universe (www.auctionuniverse. com) will process card transactions for sellers.

- *Deal with auction houses that offer a guarantee.* Some of the larger auction houses, like Sotheby's and Christie's, will guarantee the items they sell online. Make sure you read the guarantee to see if there's any dollar limit.

- *Beware of shills.* Shills are decoy bidders. They have no intention of buying but simply bid in collusion with the seller to heat up the auction and the price. You should stick with Web sites that prohibit sellers from bidding on their own merchandise. Most sites ban this practice.

  If, however, a seller is having his friends bid, you have no way of knowing. eBay has security policies to catch shills and will ban repeat offenders. But catching shills is difficult. Your best defense is to know the value of what you're buying, place a limit on what you'll pay (and stick to it), and increase your bids by low increments.

- *Don't worry about missing a purchase.* If something comes up at auction that you really want and the bids go over your limit, don't worry. A similar item is sure to be on sale in the near future.

$CROOGE INVESTING TIP #106

Save $1000s by Getting Your Auction Catalogs Online

It used to be you could go broke just subscribing to auction catalogs. Christie's and Sotheby's, for example, generally charge $30 to $50 each for their catalogs. If you subscribed to catalogs of 150 of the major auction houses, it would cost you $75,000 to $100,000 a year just to get the catalogs mailed to you.

Now you can get these catalogs online for free. Interactive Collector provides access to about 5000 catalogs from the world's leading auction houses on its Web site, www.icollector.com.

$CROOGE INVESTING TIP #107

When You Sell, Consider Not Setting a Minimum Bid

Most of the advice so far has been to bidders wanting to buy something cheap through Internet auction sites. But what about when you want to sell? Many experienced sellers on the Internet choose not to set a minimum bid, because it discourages buyers. Amazingly, in most cases, bidding is fast and furious on items that have no minimum bid, and the price quickly rises to fair market value, or even higher. Take a chance on smaller items until you feel comfortable using this strategy.

$CROOGE INVESTING TIP #108

Don't Buy Manufactured Rarities

There may be a few exceptions, but generally, limited-edition collector items such as coins, plates, and artwork aren't even worth looking at. These are manufactured on assembly lines by direct marketing firms and sold at high prices. They're usually not worth it. Despite the advertisers' claims, for most of these items, there isn't a large enough collector base to support the high prices. Wait a couple of years and you'll be able to go to a secondhand store or the Internet auction sites and buy the same piece for a fraction of the original offering price.

$CROOGE INVESTING TIP #109

Don't Buy New Issues of Commemorative and Proof Coins

Writing in *Barron's,* R.W. Bradford, editor of the coin newsletter *Analysis & Outlook,* has shown that nearly all the coins sold by the U.S. Mint have been terrible investments. A few issues have done well, such as one of the lower-mintage Olympic sets, but more than 90 percent of the new issues sold by the U.S. Mint have fallen below their initial offering price within a few years of their minting. I've found this to be true with many issues of foreign commemorative coins as well.

You're better off avoiding all new commemorative and collector coins when they're first issued. If you want to own the coin, wait a year or two and buy it in the secondary market. Chances are you'll pay a lot less for it.

Free Sample! Bradford publishes one of the better newsletters on the rare coin market. Like me, he has a Scrooge mentality and is always trying to steer his readers from the overpriced items and into the overlooked bargains. I've arranged for you to get a free sample copy of his newsletter, *R.W. Bradford's Analysis & Outlook,* P.O. Box 1167, Port Townsend, WA 98368. It's regularly $78 a year for 12 issues.

14

SLASHING FEES ON OFF-SHORE INVESTMENTS AND FOREIGN CURRENCIES

> Merchants have no country.
>
> —*Thomas Jefferson*

SOMETIMES THE SCROOGE INVESTOR also wants to be the "private international investor," keeping his or her funds confidential in Swiss bank accounts, offshore property, and safe deposit boxes. This chapter offers a variety of helpful tips on investing offshore.

Investing offshore presents its own particular problems to the cost-conscious investor. Some foreign banks charge high fees—higher than U.S. banks. Discount brokerage firms are not as prevalent in foreign countries. No-load funds are not nearly as popular in foreign countries as they are in the United States. And converting dollars into foreign currencies can be expensive. Yet despite these difficulties, you can cut costs when investing offshore.

$CROOGE INVESTING TIP #110

How to Invest in Foreign Currencies and Get the Interbank Rate! (or Very Close to It)

If you buy foreign currencies as investments, you might pay as much as 3 to 7 percent over the spot price if you buy the banknotes themselves. You can cut that charge to less than 1 percent by getting the interbank rate, the same rate large institutions and foreign currency traders enjoy. The method is simple: Invest in foreign currencies through Firstar Bank's international currency programs.

Firstar offers several different accounts in a variety of currencies: World Currency Access Interest Account, which offers money market rates in 25 currencies, and international certificates of deposit (ICDs) in 25 currencies. Currencies include the euro, German deutsche mark, Japanese yen, Swiss franc, British pound, French franc, and Canadian dollar.

The minimum investment varies—$2500 for a World Currency Access Interest Account and $10,000 for ICDs in major currencies. The ICDs are available for terms of three, six, nine, and 12 months. There is no charge to roll them over, but you will pay a foreign exchange fee each time you renew an ICD.

A new product offered by Firstar is the WorldCurrency Index CD. This allows you to hold a diversified index of foreign currencies. The first one available, Series 1, holds four different currencies in equal parts: the Australian dollar, Hong Kong dollar, Mexican peso, and EMU euro. For a deposit of six months to a year, you'll earn an interest rate of 7 percent, considerably higher than the 4 percent the bank is currently offering for U.S. dollar-denominated CDs of the same maturity. You could also have a capital gain or loss should the currencies in the index rise or fall while you're holding the CD.

Firstar offers several great ways to have a low-cost foreign currency account without going abroad. The accounts are also insured up to $100,000 by the Federal Deposit Insurance Corporation, just like any other bank account. However, the insurance doesn't protect you against any principal that you lose due to price fluctuations in the foreign currencies you hold.

For more information, contact Firstar International Markets, P.O. Box 524, Tram 20-5, St. Louis, MO 63130; 1-800-926-4922 or 1-314-418-0292; www.mercantile.com.

$CROOGE INVESTING TIP #111

How to Get the Best Rate on Foreign Currencies in Small Amounts or When You Travel

Depending on the currency, the location, and the vendor, you could pay anywhere from 1 to 7 percent over the bank rate for foreign currency. The best way to get small amounts of foreign currency is to buy through banks, not through currency dealers. You also get a better rate for traveler's checks than you do for cash. And you usually get the best rate when you use your credit card (although see Tip #113).

You'll usually get a better exchange rate in the country in which the currency circulates than you will in a different country. For example, if you're buying British pounds, you'll get a better rate in London than you will in Paris, Amsterdam, or New York. Use vacation trips to stock up on currencies.

And don't forget: Banks and exchange dealers will *not* convert *coins* into foreign currency. So keep your coins to a minimum. Plan on donating them to charity or giving them away as gifts to children or interested collectors.

$CROOGE INVESTING TIP #112

Learn How to Shop Smart for Currencies

If you're buying currencies, it pays to shop around. Here are my best recommendations:

- *Try your local banks.* Large commercial banks, particularly in big cities, often have a foreign-exchange department. Small banks often charge more.

- *Find out the total cost, after all expenses.* Always ask for the total price. Say to them, "I need 10,000 Swiss francs. How much, in total, will those cost me?" Make sure there are no other charges.

- *Get prices from more than one dealer.* Call several, one right after the other. All of them can accommodate anyone, anywhere in the country, whether you're buying cash, traveler's checks, or wiring funds.

Following are some of the best sources for foreign currency:

- **Asset Strategies International** (1700 Rockville Pike, Suite 400, Rockville, MD 20852; 800-831-0007 or 301-881-8600; www.assetstrategies.com) offers foreign traveler's checks in seven currencies at very low prices, plus the ability to make electronic transfers of funds abroad.

- **American Automobile Association (AAA)** offers commission-free American Express traveler's checks to its members. Some AAA travel agencies also offer them commission-free to their clients. They are offered in five currencies, but if you're buying in any currency other than the U.S. dollar, you will pay a fee for the currency conversion. Check the white pages of your telephone directory for the AAA office nearest you.

- **Thomas Cook Currency Services** (41 E. 42nd St., New York, NY 10017, 800-287-7362 or 212-679-4365) offers traveler's checks in all major currencies at 110 branches through the United States. Check your local yellow pages under Foreign Exchange for the office nearest you.

- **Firstar Bank** (P.O. Box 524, Tram 20-5, St. Louis, MO 63130; 800-926-4922 or 314-418-0292) offers foreign exchange, electronic funds transfers, and a variety of foreign currency CDs, as noted above. It charges a 1 percent commission on its traveler's checks, however.

$CROOGE INVESTING TIP #113

Beware of Extra Charges When You Use Your Credit Card Abroad

Using your credit card when you travel is cheaper than using traveler's checks—or even exchanging cash—at a bank or hotel. The rate you get on credit cards and debit cards is the interbank rate, the same exchange rate big financial institutions get, which is 1 percent. That's about 5 percent below the retail rate.

However, some banks are tacking on an extra charge, a currency conversion surcharge, for foreign currency conversions. Most of those that have added this surcharge are charging between 2 and 3 percent. That's still lower than the retail rate but more than you need to pay.

Before you use any credit card overseas, read your credit card agreement, or call the issuing bank's customer service line and find out if they have a currency conversion surcharge and how much it is. Currently, American Express and Diner's Club are still charging only 1 percent. If your bank is tacking on these charges, find a new credit card for your foreign travel.

$CROOGE INVESTING TIP #114

Choose From Among Three Low-Cost Foreign Banks for American Investors

Over the years, I've recommended three foreign banks that have a long tradition of catering to American investors. They are:

1. **Lloyds Bank Worldwide Service** (P.O. Box 349, 1 Waterloo Place, London SW1Y 5NJ, England, 011-

44-171-839-2099), one of the largest banks in the
world, offers a unique service to U.S. and foreign
investors: a "high-interest cheque account" that pays
interest ranging from 1.5 to 3 percent. You receive a
checkbook, a special VISA card that allows you to
make purchases anywhere in the world, and a cash
withdrawal card. The account is denominated in
British pounds. Minimum investment is only $2500.
Larger amounts are required if you wish to buy and
sell securities.

2. **Anglo-Irish Bank (Austria)** (P.O. Box 306, A-1011
Vienna, Austria, 011-431-406-61-61) is a favorite for
cost-conscious investors. Minimum investment to
open an account is only $5000. The Anglo-Irish Bank
(Austria) specializes in buying and selling mutual
funds and charges only 1 percent commission. They
also offer accounts in stocks, bonds, certificates of
deposit, and precious metals.

3. **Hong Kong & Shanghai Bank** (1 Queen's Road
Central, Hong Kong) offers the most flexible and
high-yielding multicurrency accounts in the world. Its
CombiNations Savings Accounts are offered in 10
different currencies, including the Swiss franc, euro,
U.S. dollar, and Japanese yen. Minimum investment is
only $1000.

A note on Swiss banks: I've recommended many Swiss
banks over the years, but for a variety of reasons, Swiss
banks have recently become less hospitable toward U.S.
investors. For example, Ueberseebank in Zurich used to
encourage accounts from U.S. investors, but it no longer
does since being bought out by AIG, the large insurance
company. If you want a Swiss bank account, the best
approach is to visit a branch of one of the large Swiss banks
in Zurich or Geneva (Swiss Bank Corporation, CreditSuisse,
Bank Leu). It is much easier for an American to open a Swiss

franc savings account or other type of account in person than by mail.

An excellent book on Swiss banks is *Swiss Bank Accounts: A Personal Guide to Ownership, Benefits, and Use*. It's by Michael Arthur Jones, a U.S. accountant. You can order it from McGraw-Hill, P.O. Box 182604, Columbus, OH 43272; 800-262-4729; $24.95 plus handling.

$CROOGE INVESTING TIP #115

Here's the Best Low-Cost Way to Hold Precious Metals in Switzerland

One of the best ways to hold precious metals offshore is through ScotiaMocatta Delivery Orders (SMDOs).

ScotiaMocatta certificates are nonnegotiable warehouse receipts for gold (or silver) stored safely in your own name in Zurich, Switzerland. According to tax experts, the metals certificate is not considered a foreign bank account, so there is no need to report its existence. Because you send funds to a domestic dealer (see below), there's no requirement to report money sent overseas. Because the certificates are nonnegotiable, you can carry them in and out of the United States without having to declare them to customs.

ScotiaMocatta Delivery Orders are available for gold bullion coins in units of 10 American Eagles, 10 Canadian Maple Leafs, 10 Austrian Philamonicas, 10 Mexican 50 Pesos, or 10 Austrian (or Hungarian) Coronas. If you prefer gold bullion to coins, bars are available in 100 or 400 troy ounces. Silver units are available in 500 one-ounce silver Eagles, 400 one-ounce silver Canadian Maple Leafs, or ten 100-ounce bars.

Using these warehouse receipts, you can present your certificate in Zurich and take delivery of your gold or silver if you wish. It's a taxable event only if you sell your gold or silver, not if you take delivery. Your stored metals are insured by Lloyd's of London. The charge is 0.05 percent per annum for storage and insurance. That's slightly more than some

Swiss banks charge for storing metals, but I believe the extra benefits are well worth the small added cost. In fact, 0.05 percent is a real bargain for storing silver, which is bulky and requires substantial storage space.

You can obtain ScotiaMocatta Delivery Orders from six reputable dealers in the United States:

- Asset Strategies International: 1-800-831-0007; 1-301-881-8600; www.assetstrategies.com.

- Blanchard & Co: 1-800-285-5466; 1-504-837-3010; www.blanchardonline.com.

- Camino Coins: 1-800-348-8001; 1-650-348-3000.

- Centennial Precious Metals: 1-800-869-5115; 1-303-393-0322.

- Dillon-Gage Metals Division: 1-800-375-4653; 1-214-788-4765; www.dillongage.com.

- Hancock & Harwell: 1-800-995-6566; 1-404-261-6565; www.raregold.com.

Note: Since prices can range widely among dealers, you are better off if you get price quotes from at least three different dealers before buying. Call them one right after the other and see which one will give you the best price.

$CROOGE INVESTING TIP #116

Store Your Gold, Silver, Platinum, and Palladium for FREE in Australia in This Government-Guaranteed Program

The Perth Mint in Australia has recently begun offering a storage program for precious metals. In many ways, it's similar to the ScotiaMocatta Delivery Orders listed above. The minimum investment is much higher—$25,000. With Scotia-Mocatta the minimum is not a stated dollar amount but a certain amount of coins or bars of a certain weight. If you bought ScotiaMocatta's minimum of 10 gold coins at about $300 for each coin, then you would only have to invest $3000 to meet the minimum. There is another difference between the two programs. With ScotiaMocatta the metal is stored nonfungibly, i.e., each person's metal is stored separately in the vault and is not comingled with metals belonging to other depositors. Perth Mint also offers a nonfungible storage option. However, it charges higher storage fees in its nonfungible storage program than ScotiaMocatta does.

Many people prefer nonfungible storage because it's considered to be a smidgen safer, especially if the issuing company goes bankrupt. With fungible storage, you would, in all likelihood, get your metals in a bankruptcy, but there could be a delay while records are sorted out. With nonfungible storage, it's much clearer who owns what.

Since the Perth Mint is owned by the western government of Australia, bankruptcy or fraud isn't likely. The safety of your precious metal holdings is "government guaranteed," whether you use the fungible or the nonfungible storage program. However, you can only get the free storage in the fungible (i.e., comingled) program.

Perth is also cheaper than ScotiaMocatta in the certificate fee it charges. ScotiaMocatta charges $100 per certificate; Perth $50. However, Perth's is based on the transaction; ScotiaMocatta's certificates are preprinted and based on minimum purchases. This can make Perth an even better deal for larger investors. For example, if you wanted to buy $100,000 worth of one-ounce gold coins at $300 each, you would have to buy 18 preprinted SMDOs (20 coins each) for a total cost of $1800. With Perth, you would only have to buy one certificate at a total cost of $50. Scrooge Investors, take notice.

What it boils down to is this: For larger investors, Perth Mint is the lowest-cost; for smaller investors, ScotiaMocatta is the only way to go.

Only one company currently sells the Perth Mint Certificates (although more could be on board by the time this book is published). For more information, call or write Asset

Strategies International, 1700 Rockville Pike, Suite 400, Rockville, MD 20852; 1-800-831-0007 or 1-301-881-8600; www.assetstrategies.com.

$CROOGE INVESTING TIP #117

For Larger Investors, Consider Liechtenstein for a Lower-Profile (Though *Not* Lower-Cost) Alternative to Switzerland

For larger investors, Mike Ketcher, editor of *The Financial Privacy Report,* recommends Liechtenstein. But he warns that these are *not* low-cost banks. Their charges rival those of neighboring Switzerland. However, they offer more privacy than even Swiss banks. Unlike Switzerland, Liechtenstein has no tax treaty or mutual legal assistance treaty with the United States. It's where the Swiss people themselves go when they want financial privacy.

Because Liechtenstein banks cater to the very wealthy, many of them have high-minimum investments. Some of them won't even open accounts for anyone with a U.S. address. However, for about US$10 to US$15 a month, you can get a Canadian mailing address at any Mail Boxes, Etc., in Toronto or Vancouver and have your bank statements forwarded to you.

Some of Liechtenstein's leading banks are:

- **Liechtenstein Landesbank** (FL-9490 Vaduz, Stadtle 44, Postfach 384, Liechtenstein; Phone: 011-41-75-236-8811). It has no stated minimums in its literature, except for managed accounts: $250,000.

- **Neue Bank** (Kirchstrasse 8, Postfach 1533, FL-9490 Vaduz; Phone: 011-41-75-236-0808). Minimum: SFr 50,000 (about $35,000). You can get a CD for a minimum of SFr 5000 ($3500).

- **VP Bank** (In Zentrum, FL-9490 Vaduz; Phone: 011-41-75-235-6655). Minimums are $100,000; $500,000 for managed accounts. VP Bank also has a branch in the

British Virgin Islands, a privacy and tax haven in the Caribbean. For information, write or call VP Bank (BVI), 65 Main St., P.O. Box 3463, Road Town, Tortola, British Virgin Islands. Phone: 1-284-494-1100.

$CROOGE INVESTING TIP #118

For Swiss-Style Banking at a Fraction of the Cost, Go to Austria
In 1995, Anglo Irish Bank acquired an Austrian bank that had been in existence for over a century. For many years, this bank has provided excellent service to an English-speaking clientele, including brokerage services, mutual funds, precious metals, foreign currency CDs, and managed accounts.

Minimum deposits range from $25,000 for a basic savings account in any freely convertible currency and $50,000 for a securities account (which includes a VISA or Euro/Master credit card) to $100,000 for investment advisory and portfolio management services and $500,000 for an account with a personal manager. Costs are reasonable and generally lower than you'll find at Swiss banks.

For more information, write or call Anglo Irish Bank, Rathausstrasse 20, P.O. Box 306, A-1011 Vienna, Austria. Phone: 011-431-406-61-61.

$CROOGE INVESTING TIP #119

For Small Investors, the Channel Islands or the Isle of Man May Be Best
If you want to open a small foreign account, the best place to go may be the Channel Islands or the Isle of Man. These countries have a tradition of banking and business confidentiality. You can earn interest comparable to what you would earn at a bank in the United States. Costs are generally lower than banks in Switzerland and Liechtenstein.

There are also building societies, which are the United Kingdom's equivalent to savings and loans in the United States. Sometimes you can open an account at one of these for as little as $300.

The following are recommended by international adviser
Gary Scott, editor of *Gary Scott's World Reports:*

Alliance & Leicester, P.O. Box 226, 10-12 Prospect
Hill, Douglas, Isle of Man, IM991RY; Phone: 011-
44-1624-663566.

Anglo Irish Bank (Isle of Man), 69 Athol St., Douglas,
Isle of Man IM1 1JE; Phone: 011-44-1624-625508.

Birmingham-Midshires, P.O. Box 106, Canada Court,
St. Peter Port, Guernsey, Channel Islands, GY1
3ER; Phone: 011-44-1481-700680.

Portman Channel Islands, Oliver Court, Oliver Street,
St. Ann, Aldernay, Channel Islands, GY9 3EF;
Phone: 011-44-1481-822747.

$CROOGE INVESTING TIP #120

For Swiss Banking in the Bahamas, Try Nordfinanz

Swiss banks have some of the highest fees in the world.
However, one Swiss bank with reasonable fees is Nordfinanz Bank. It has a branch in the Bahamas. It offers accounts
in foreign currencies, precious metals, stocks and bonds, and
has managed accounts. However, Nordfinanz has recently
raised its minimum account size to $100,000. If you are still
interested, write Nordfinanz Bank Zurich, Nassau Branch,
Norfolk House, Frederick Street, P.O. Box N-7529, Nassau,
the Bahamas.

$CROOGE INVESTING TIP #121

Use This Offshore VISA Debit Card to Get the Interbank Rate at ATMs, Hotels, and Restaurants on All Your Foreign Travel

At some foreign banks, you can open an account for as little
as $2000—and get a VISA debit card. You can use the debit
card at any ATM machine, anywhere in the world, and you'll
receive the Interbank rate for any currency conversion. These

are checking accounts that pay interest comparable to what you might earn on a U.S. dollar-denominated money market account. The account can be denominated in U.S. dollars or British pounds. Unless you spend a lot of time in Great Britain, you're probably better off having it denominated in U.S. dollars.

Besides the lowest foreign exchange rates, you also get privacy. Your debit card won't appear on any credit reports, and your transaction records won't be as readily available to snoops as they are in the United States.

Two highly regarded offshore banks offer VISA debit cards for modest investments of $2000–$5000 minimum. They are:

> Cater Allen Bank (Jersey) Limited, P.O. Box 476, Cater Allen House, Commercial Street, St. Helier, Jersey JE4 8WU Channel Islands; Phone: 011-1534-828-000.

> Lloyds Bank PLC, P.O. Box 12 Peveril Buildings, Peveril Square, Douglas, Isle of Man IM99 1SS. 011-44-1624-638104. Also, as mentioned earlier, Lloyds Bank Worldwide Service (P.O. Box 349, 1 Waterloo Place, London SW1Y 5NJ, 011-44-171-839-2099) offers a similar VISA debit card with a minimum of $2500.

$CROOGE INVESTING TIP #122

Subscribe to *The Financial Times* at Half Price

The best way to keep abreast of foreign markets, offshore funds, and other international news is through *The Financial Times,* a daily newspaper (six days a week). It normally sells for $368 a year, but you can save 50 percent off the regular rates. Typically, it offers an introductory price of $184. Call 1-800-628-8808 (or if outside the United States, 212-752-4500). Say you're a new subscriber and ask for the introductory rate. You can get lots of free information, without subscribing, at its Web site: www.ft.com.

The Financial Times lists daily hundreds of offshore investment trusts (mutual funds), with addresses and telephone numbers for further information.

$CROOGE INVESTING TIP #123

Get Information on Offshore Investing Through Specialized Web Sites and Newsletters

John Dessauer publishes a monthly newsletter called *Investor's World* (Phillips Publishing, 7811 Montrose Rd., Potomac, MD 20854; 800-777-5005). It's $149 a year for 12 issues plus hotline.

Gary Scott publishes a good newsletter on foreign investments, *Gary Scott's World Reports* (International Service Center, 3106 Tamiami Trail North, Naples, FL 34103; 941-261-1222; www.gary-scott.com).

ADR.com (www.adr.com) is a great place to research American Depositary Receipts (foreign stocks that trade on U.S. stock exchanges).

Central Europe Online (www.invest.centraleurope.com) will give you info on the markets in this part of the world. You can lurk on the message boards or sign up for the free daily e-mail newsletter.

Currency Trends (www.updatenews.com) tracks currencies, forecasts trends, and gives recommendations on positions. A monthly subscription is a whopping $600, but you can get a four-week free trial.

Emerging Markets Companion (www.emgmkts.com) is free and contains lots of news and research from around the world. It's updated frequently.

Euromoney Online (www.emwl.com) is the Web site of this leading European financial magazine. The entire issue is available on the Web site.

Far Eastern Economic Review (www.feer.com) gives you oodles of free articles and ads from this Hong Kong–based magazine.

Imoney is a Web site for those interested in Canadian investments. Go to www.imoney.com. You can learn about everything from the wild and woolly Vancouver Stock Exchange to Canadian tax-free retirement accounts.

Latinvestor (www.latinvestor.com) is a Web site for those wishing to invest in Latin America. Unfortunately, much of the information on the site is in Spanish.

Micropal (www.micropal.com) gives you daily and weekly data on 38,000 mutual funds, including many offshore funds. While the Web site offers various subscription databases and software, running into the thousands of dollars, you can get lots of information free.

Nikkei Net Interactive (www.nni.nikkei.com.jp) is a Web site sponsored by *The Nikkei Weekly,* Japan's English-language business newspaper. You'll find a wealth of information on this site, including a database of over 3000 publicly traded Japanese companies. Unfortunately, you'll have to pay about $50 for a six-month subscription.

Worldly Investor (www.worldlyinvestor.com) offers a free newsletter containing business and financial news from every corner of the earth.

PART 4

MORE SCROOGE INVESTING

15

LOW-COST METHODS
OF BORROWING MONEY

Want to make a million dollars? Borrow a million and pay it off!

—Jack Miller

I T'S NOT WISE to borrow too much money for anything, but people constantly overborrow through their credit cards, automobile purchases, real estate, and sometimes even when investing in stocks or commodities. Overleveraging got Donald Trump in trouble, though he's making a comeback. Anybody can become a millionaire on paper, if she borrows enough money. Just be *prudent;* that's what Uncle Scrooge would say. Borrow only when the odds are strongly in your favor. True Scrooges build real wealth, not just paper wealth!

$CROOGE INVESTING TIP #124

Before You Borrow Money, Go to This Web Site

When you're applying for credit, it pays to shop around and to know the market. There's an easy way to do this on the Internet.

Whether you're applying for a credit card, mortgage loan, home equity loan, small business loan, auto loan, or personal loan, you can find the lowest rates at the Web site www.bankrate.com. This Web site gives you rates from 3500 institutions in hundreds of cities across the country. You can also learn about how to check your credit report, determine hidden costs and fees, and manage your debt.

$CROOGE INVESTING TIP #125

Before You Apply for a Loan, One Simple Step Could Reduce Your Interest Rate and Maybe Even Keep You From Getting Turned Down
Your credit rating could affect the interest rate you'll pay and perhaps even your ability to get a loan. Don't assume your credit rating is good. Over 40 percent of credit reports have errors. Many more have outdated information. Nevertheless, lenders often look only on your credit report to determine your suitability for a loan.

Fortunately, you can correct your credit report. If you have a dispute with a lender, you often can insert an explanation into your credit report, giving your side of the story. Before you get a loan, or at least once a year even if you're not getting a loan, you should obtain and review a copy of your credit report from each of the Big Three credit reporting agencies. The cost varies from free up to $8, depending on which agency you're dealing with and which state you live in. To find out the procedure, call or write to each of them:

> Equifax
> P.O. Box 740241
> Atlanta, GA 30374
> 1-800-685-1111
> www.equifax.com
>
> Experian (formerly TRW)
> P.O. Box 2104
> Allen, TX 75013
> 1-800-682-7654
> www.experian.com

Trans Union Corporation
760 W. Sproul Road
Springfield, PA 19064
1-800-888-4213

$CROOGE INVESTING TIP #126

The Best Source for Low-Cost Funds? YOUR DISCOUNT BROKER.
Want to borrow below the prime rate? Try your stockbroker.
Stockbrokers will lend money at the broker's call rate. It's
usually about 0.5 to 1 percent below the prime rate, which is
the rate at which banks lend money to their best corporate
customers.

All you need to do to borrow at the broker's call rate is to
have marginable securities in a margin account. The brokers
listed in Chapters 7 and 8 offer margin accounts. Simply fill
out their forms, and you can borrow money against the securities in your account. But don't overdo it. You can borrow up
to 50 percent of the market value of your securities, but
remember, if the price of your stocks goes down, you will
have less to borrow and could even get a margin call, forcing
you to put up more money or securities.

$CROOGE INVESTING TIP #127

**Seven Ways to Raise a Down Payment on Real Estate (for the Cash-Poor
Investor)**
If you can't accumulate enough capital to raise a down payment, here are some creative possibilities you may not be
aware of:

- *Lease with an option to buy.* Just make sure you get a
  rent credit toward the downpayment.
- If you or your spouse is eligible, *get a VA mortgage that
  requires no downpayment.*
- *Get a VA mortgage with a low downpayment.*

- *Buy a foreclosed VA or FHA home* that requires no downpayment or only a low downpayment.

- When dealing with an investor, *get a second mortgage note* for all or part of the downpayment money you need. Negotiate a favorable interest rate.

- *Offer some unnecessary item as a downpayment,* such as a second car, boat, or RV.

- *Try a share-equity downpayment.* Some real estate brokers and mortgage companies are linking well-heeled investors with cash-strapped homebuyers. Both parties benefit. The buyer has someone to share the downpayment; the investor shares in any increase in home values and may collect additional fees.

$CROOGE INVESTING TIP #128

Consider a Low-Cost Home Equity Loan

Interest rates on home equity loans are higher than the prime rate, but most banks are eliminating closing costs on these loans. Also, rates are much lower than credit cards, and you can deduct the interest. Shop around for the best rate, starting at your credit union (if you belong to one), where loans are generally cheaper (although maturities may be shorter and the credit line smaller).

Also check the Web site www.bankrate.com for the best home equity deals. Be sure to note all the expenses involved, not just the official interest rate.

$CROOGE INVESTING TIP #129

Borrow From Your 401(k) Plan

You can borrow against your 401(k) for any reason. It's simple, private, and cheap. You're borrowing from yourself, so you don't have to worry about intrusive paperwork or getting rejected.

You can borrow 50 percent of your account balance, up to a maximum of $50,000. No minimum is required. If your account balance is under $10,000, you can borrow the entire amount, but you must provide collateral to the extent that your loan exceeds 50 percent of the account balance.

The interest rate is generally a couple of percentage points higher than the prime rate. You'll also have to pay off the loan in five years, making payments quarterly. It's repaid through automatic deductions from your paycheck. Check with your company for details.

$CROOGE INVESTING TIP #130

As a Last Resort, Tap Your Credit Cards

Using your credit card to get funds for an investment or consumer purchase is one step away from going to the pawnbroker or loan shark. Interest rates are usually above 18 percent. Rates are often even higher for cash advances and cash-advance checks. Don't do it unless it's absolutely necessary, and if you do, make sure that you use the lowest-interest credit card you can find. You can get up-to-date lists of credit cards with no annual fees and with the lowest rates at either of these Web sites: www.bankrate.com or www.cardtrak.com.

Some platinum cards will charge you only a 3.9 percent introductory rate for a full year on all balance transfers. Be wary of cash advance fees (usually around 3 percent, charged immediately).

$CROOGE INVESTING TIP #131

Look for Low-Fee or No-Fee Cash Advances on Credit Cards

In past editions of *Scrooge Investing,* I have highlighted VISA, MasterCard, and other credit cards (including the Discover card) that offer cash advances and cash-advance checks with a normal 25-day grace period. In essence, they are giving you a short-term, interest-free personal loan. However, I know of no such programs currently. (If new ones become available, I'll update this information on my Web site, www.forecasts-strategies.com under "Scrooge Investing.")

The best low-cost cash-advance program is offered by AT&T Universal platinum card. The Universal platinum card is linked through the MasterCard network, so the card can be used practically anywhere. The card currently charges a 3 percent transaction fee (or $5, whichever is greater) when you use a cash advance or convenience check, but the charge is limited to a *maximum of $25* per transaction! To keep your costs of borrowing down, it pays to borrow substantial sums.

AT&T charges you the maximum $25 fee but does not charge additional interest fees until after the 25-day grace period.

Note: AT&T Universal platinum card may change its fee schedule on its cash advances and convenience checks at any time, so check with them before acting on this advice.

$CROOGE INVESTING TIP #132

Use Credit Cards That Give You Rewards and Rebates

Several credit cards offer rebates—up to 5 percent—on purchases you make. And remember, as Benjamin Franklin once said, "a nickel saved is a nickel earned" (quote updated to account for inflation). There are several excellent cashback cards available, the best offering no annual fee and no cap on rewards.

• **Discover** had one of the first rebate cards available, and it's still one of the best. Its platinum card, issued in 1999, offers a cash rebate similar to its original card. However, it also offers double points with some retailers (1-800-347-2683).

    And if you use your card to shop on Discover card's Internet ShopCenter, you can sometimes earn additional bonuses for any purchases you make. You can also access your account information online and even pay your Discover card bill online through their SmartCheck payment option.

- **American Express** rolled out a no-fee, cash-back Optima card in 1999, which is ideal if you charge large amounts during the year. It pays you back 1.5 percent on purchases over $5000. If you don't use your credit card as much, try the GE Rewards MasterCard (1-800-437-3927), which pays you 1 percent after you've charged $2000 in the year.

- **The Sony card,** issued by Citibank (1-800-748-7669), pays you 1 percent back on general purchases, 2 percent on Sony products, and 3 percent on charges at over 1000 Sony partners, including Best Buy and Circuit City. You can even use it to buy movie tickets at Sony theaters. Unfortunately, rewards are limited to $250. There's no annual fee, though, and the interest rate is only 13.65 percent.

- **Jefferson Bank's Smart VISA** (1-800-768-9668) pays you 1 percent, but it charges a $25 annual fee.

- If you buy on the Internet, then you might like the **Yahoo!VISA card** issued by First USA. It offers a 1 percent reward, which you can redeem with certain online merchants. First USA also offers the e.card, which has a fixed interest rate of 9.99 percent, no annual fee, and a 5 percent cash rebate at a dozen popular Internet sites, including Amazon.com and e-toys.com. There's also no cap on rewards.

$CROOGE INVESTING TIP #133

If You Carry a Credit Card Balance, Stick With the Lowest-Rate Cards
Cash-rebate cards work best for those who pay off their credit cards every month. If you carry a balance, you're much better off with a card offering the lowest interest rate. Here are several cards that are always among the lowest-rate cards.

USAA Savings (1-800-922-9092) charges the prime rate plus 1 percent (currently 8.75 percent), with an annual fee of $45. Pulaski Bank & Trust charges the discount rate plus 4.95 percent (currently 9.45 percent) and a $50 annual fee. Simmons's Bank (1-800-636-5151) rate is the discount rate plus 5 percent (currently 9.5 percent), with a $50 annual fee.

$CROOGE INVESTING TIP #134

Don't Let Them Sock You With a Late-Payment Fee

If you're late making a payment by just one day, many credit card companies sock you with a late-payment fee of up to $50! That's outrageous.

Not only that, but even one late payment appearing on your credit report can cause your rates to rise on other credit cards you own. Credit card issuers are using late payments as an excuse to raise rates, because they interpret a late payment as evidence that you're a greater credit risk.

What utter nonsense. I travel a lot, and I sometimes miss a payment because I'm out of town when the bill is due. So my payment reaches the credit card issuer late. What's more, sometimes even if you mail your payment a week ahead of the due date, the credit card issuer may claim that it didn't receive it in time.

Here's how you can protect yourself from this scheme by the credit card issuers.

First, make sure you pay your credit card bills as soon as they come in. Second, if the bills always come in at a time in the month when cash is tight, then call the issuer and change the due date. Third, if you're hit with one of these big late-payment fees, complain loudly to the credit card issuer. Say that it's outrageous and you want it taken off your bill. In my experience, if you complain, the penalty will be removed.

You won't find many credit card issuers these days who don't charge late fees. The only ones I've heard of are credit unions, but you have to be a member of the credit union to take advantage of it. If you do belong to a credit union, see if it offers any credit cards that have no late payment charge.

The smallest late payment charge I've seen is about $20. The Hawaii National Bank in Honolulu has a credit card that charges a late fee of 5 percent of the minimum payment due, which would likely be a low charge. If interested, call 1-808-528-7711.

$CROOGE INVESTING TIP #135

If You Get in Over Your Head, Go to These Organizations
Credit is so easy that getting into debt can become a vicious cycle: you borrow more money just to pay the interest on the money you've already borrowed. Be careful. Successful investors learn to live within their means.

But if your debt gets out of hand, then you will need to negotiate with lenders for easier payment terms, budget your expenses, and get your debts paid off as quickly as possible.

Avoid credit-repair firms that advertise on television or in the local newspaper. They often make matters worse. If you need help, go to one of the several nonprofit organizations designed to help people manage their debt. The following organizations can help you:

American Credit Counseling
1-800-769-3571
www.debtfree.org

Consolidated Credit Counseling Services
1-800-728-3632
www.debtfree.org

Debt Counselors of America
1-800-680-3328
www.getoutofdebt.org

National Foundation for Consumer Credit
1-800-388-2227
www.nfcc.org

CHAPTER 16

CUTTING YOUR BIGGEST INVESTMENT COSTS—TAXES!

There will never be a tax law without legal loopholes.

—Larry Abraham

EVERY COST-CONSCIOUS SCROOGE INVESTOR faces four major enemies: bad investment advice, high fees and commissions, inflation, and taxes. Investors worldwide recognize that taxes can easily be the highest portfolio expense. U.S. investors have seen inflation cut the value of their portfolios by as much as 10 percent a year. But federal and state taxes routinely take a much bigger bite, 40 percent or more, depending on where you live.

Complying with the tax code also costs you money. Taxes are now so complicated that you almost have to hire a professional tax preparer just to make sure you're filling out your tax return properly.

One of the worst problems facing investors is the taxation of phantom income. This irksome situation occurs frequently with holders of certificates of deposit (CDs), zero-coupon bonds, and mutual funds. Let's face it, Uncle Sam is no friend of investors.

MANY WAYS TO BEAT UNCLE SAM

But wait! Loopholes abound in even the most complex and onerous tax system in history. Fortunately, the IRS permits several methods of beating taxes. Unfortunately, these loopholes are sometimes so complicated that you practically have to be a CPA to figure them out.

For example, investors can take advantage of the latest developments in individual retirement accounts (IRAs), like the Roth IRA. The new capital gains rates passed in 1997 also are a blessing for investors. Here, they've complicated things unnecessarily by having four different marginal tax rates for capital gains.

Uncle Sam interferes with Uncle Scrooge's investment plans so much that Scrooge is likely to find better opportunities in Asia, Europe, and other places, where the investment atmosphere is more conducive to making money. Germany's capital gains tax is simpler than that of the United States. It still has a long-term capital gains rate of zero.

Here are a few tax-advantaged investment vehicles and strategies you might consider.

SCROOGE INVESTING TIP #136

Prefer Individual Stocks to Managed Stock Market Mutual Funds

Mutual fund managers rarely pay attention to the tax consequences of their transactions on behalf of the fund. Their main job is pumping up the total return numbers. They'll often make short-term trades, which are taxed at the highest capital gains tax rate (39.6 percent). A tax-conscious investor would be far less likely to make such a trade, but would wait until the stock qualifies for the lower, long-term capital gains rate.

In fact, a typical diversified U.S. stock fund turns over about 80 percent of its portfolio annually. Said another way, the average stock market mutual fund holds a stock for just around 13 to 14 months. You can find out what the turnover ratio is from your fund's prospectus or by calling. If it's higher than 25 percent, then consider changing. Index funds have low turnover ratios and are therefore tax-advantaged investments. See Chapter 5 for a list of index funds.

Another alternative is to own your stock market mutual funds in a tax-advantaged account, like an IRA. That way, you won't have to worry about paying the taxes.

$CROOGE INVESTING TIP #137

Buy Low-Turnover Bond Funds

Bond funds, by the way, have even higher turnovers than managed stock funds. According to the mutual fund tracking organization Morningstar, the average turnover rate is an astounding 175 percent per year (with an average five-year total return of only 37 percent). That's outrageous. You're better off with a low-turnover bond fund. Not only will you pay less in taxes, you'll get much better returns. Some of the best funds include:

> **Enterprise Government Securities A** (1-800-432-4320), with a turnover rate of only 8 percent and a five-year total return of 45 percent through mid-1999.

> **Rushmore U.S. Government Bond** (1-800-621-7874), with a turnover rate of 49 percent and a five-year total return of 52 percent.

> **Vanguard Long-Term Bond Index** (1-800-662-7447), with a turnover rate of 57 percent and a five-year total return of 56 percent.

$CROOGE INVESTING TIP #138

Watch Out for Managed Accounts

Managed accounts also often have high turnover ratios—
even higher than mutual funds. In one recent study of 16
major brokerage firms, their model portfolios had an average annual turnover ratio of 100 percent. Stay away from
managed accounts with high turnover ratios. In fact, you
might be better off staying away from managed accounts
altogether and managing your own funds. In any case, a buy-
and-hold strategy, like that followed by billionaire investor
Warren Buffett, is much better than the "churn-and-burn"
strategies followed by most professional money managers.

$CROOGE INVESTING TIP #139

If You Don't Need Current Income From Your Investments, Opt
for Growth Stocks Over High-Dividend-Paying Stocks

If you're in the upper tax bracket and you don't need current
income, then you should prefer growth stocks to high-
dividend-paying stocks in your portfolio. The dividends on
the latter will be taxed at the top federal tax rate of 39.6 percent (plus state taxes), whereas long-term capital gains in the
growth stocks will be taxed at a maximum rate of 20 percent,
no matter what your income. Another alternative is to put
your high-income investments into a tax-advantaged account.

$CROOGE INVESTING TIP #140

Set Up a Self-Directed, IRS-Approved Pension Program

Self-directed programs include regular IRAs, Roth IRAs,
self-employed retirement accounts, and corporate pension
plans. Company-directed plans limit your choice of investments, but self-directed plans through brokerage accounts
allow maximum freedom, including foreign investments. All
income and profits are tax-deferred until you withdraw them
for retirement. And in the case of the Roth IRA, if you hold

your IRA for at least five years, all withdrawals are completely tax free.

Chapter 4 lists the best nationwide discount brokerage firms. Some of them charge an annual fee for an IRA or other self-directed retirement plan. For example, Vanguard Brokerage Services charges no transaction fee, Barry W. Murphy charges $35 a year, and Ameritrade has a whole array of charges for IRAs.

Don't be penny-wise and pound-foolish. Select the discounter that offers the best deal for all services you will need, especially commissions on trades. Because you can switch between investments all you want without tax consequences, you may be doing a lot of trading. The commissions you generate might easily exceed the annual cost of an IRA or other pension plan.

$CROOGE INVESTING TIP #141

Make the Most of Your 401(k)
Many people make the mistake of ignoring the costs and returns on their 401(k) plan and other qualified plans (plans that are associated with a corporation or other business entity).

Take management fees, for instance. Some 401(k) plans have management fees as high as 2.5 percent. However, a typical plan should be only about 1.2 percent. Unfortunately, these fees are not always well-disclosed to investors.

Then there're the investment options you have. Some plans offer dozens of funds as well as stock brokerage accounts. Many people, unfortunately, allow their company to make the choices rather than making their own choices. However, if you shop around within the funds offered by your plan, you can choose the best performers. Some plans are even starting to offer bargain-priced institutional funds, with management fees ranging from only 0.1 to 0.3 percent. That's significantly better than the 1 percent or more that many mutual funds charge.

And what if the 401(k) that your company has doesn't offer a wide range of choices or has high fees? You might be able to pressure them to upgrade the plan, especially if you've accumulated a large nest egg within the plan.

Managing your 401(k) investments isn't always easy. But there's a Web site that specializes in 401(k) issues, and it will give you a wealth of information you can use to get the most out of your 401(k) or other qualified retirement plan. Just go to www.401kafe.com. You can also find some good information at the site for the American Association for Retired Persons (www.aarp.com), although I don't think much of their politics, and the Mutual Fund Education Alliance (www. mfea.com).

$CROOGE INVESTING TIP #142

Start a Roth IRA

With a Roth IRA your money can grow tax-free, and you can take the money out tax-free during your senior years, both principal and interest. Unlike traditional IRAs, however, you can't deduct your contributions. It's not a bad tradeoff. You pay tax on your contribution now, and you avoid the tax in your declining years, when you'll most likely be in a lower tax bracket.

You just have to play by the rules. First, you can't take a tax-free distribution within five years of the first taxable year for which you made a contribution. Once you've met the five-year rule, the distribution is not taxable if it is made:

- On or after you reach age 59½
- By your beneficiary or your estate on or after your death
- After you become disabled
- For first-time home-buying expenses for you or your spouse, children, grandchildren, or ancestors

Should you convert your traditional IRA to a Roth IRA? That depends on many factors, and the calculations can get quite complicated. It's best to consult with a financial planner or a tax adviser to determine the best course of action. There's nothing wrong with starting a Roth and keeping your traditional IRA.

$CROOGE INVESTING TIP #143

Buy a Low-Cost Variable Universal Life Policy for Both Tax-Deferred Accumulation and Tax-Free Income

A low-cost variable universal life (VUL) policy could be ideal for many people. It provides (1) tax-deferred accumulation, (2) tax-free income, (3) a wide array of investment selections to corner market trends and combat inflation, (4) estate tax benefits (if you die before your investment goals are achieved, a lump-sum benefit is payable, even if death occurs in the first year your initial deposit is made).

You can even add a critical illness factor, so that if you become critically ill, you can access cash well beyond your fund value.

While VUL was introduced in the mid-eighties, it has gone through some serious consumer-oriented changes that make it even more attractive now, such enhancements as significantly lower administrative fees, a broader range of funds selections, and more life insurance benefit per dollar invested.

I used to recommend variable annuities quite strongly (see Chapter 17 on insurance), but now the variable universal life plans appear to be a lot better.

Some of the better VUL policies are offered by:

National Life, Montpelier, VT 05604; 1-800-233-4332. Their VeriTrak has over 25 investment portfolio choices and a guaranteed account for flexible planning. In addition, it has the most up-to-date riders, which can enhance an already strong product.

Manufacturers Life, 73 Tremont St., Boston, MA
02108; 1-800-VARILIN. Their new Venture VUL
boasts over 30 strategies to invest in, including a
guaranteed account. Their product design and under-
writing are their main strengths.

Southland Life, 5780 Powers Ferry Road, Atlanta, GA
30327; 1-800-872-7542. Future Dimensions is
Southland's latest and best VUL product, with over
20 funds to choose from, including six Fidelity
accounts.

Insurance specialist David T. Phillips is familiar with
these policies and can explain them in more detail and
answer any questions you may have. Call 1-800-223-9610 or
visit his Web site: www.iquote.com.

$CROOGE INVESTING TIP #144

Buy the Lowest-Cost Variable Annuities

Variable annuities are tax-deferred insured investment vehicles that allow you to invest (and trade) in a variety of investments without tax consequences. Right now, the two least
expensive variable annuity products are:

*   **Vanguard Variable Annuity Plan.** Annual fees for
    insurance and administration are approximately 0.7
    percent, substantially lower than for other annuities. It
    also has no up-front load or early withdrawal penalties.
    Choose from among 13 funds, and switch at any time
    without penalty or tax consequence. Vanguard also
    offers an international fund. Contact Vanguard Group
    of Investment Companies, P.O. Box 1103, Valley Forge,
    PA 19482; 800-522-5555.

*   **Scudder's Horizon Plan.** Annual fees are from 0.5 to
    1.50 percent, slightly higher than Vanguard's. Scudder
    offers six fund choices, including its international fund
    (1.0 percent annual fee). Contact Scudder Kemper

Investments (175 Federal St., Boston MA 02110; 800-225-2470).

$CROOGE INVESTING TIP #145

Take the Risk Out of Stock Market Investing Through Guaranteed Stock Index Annuities

Will the stock market go up or down? You know that the long-term track record of the stock market is up, but what will happen in the short term? Here's how to participate in the upside potential of the stock market without taking the investment risk. It's called the Pilot 500, a fixed, single-premium deferred annuity issued by Jefferson-Pilot Life. While there are several similar annuities linked to the S&P 500, this one is the best, according to insurance expert Andrew Westhem.

Here's how it works. The value of the S&P 500 Index on the first day of a policy year is subtracted from an average of the monthly values of the S&P 500 Index for that policy year. The difference is divided by the S&P 500 Index value on the first day of the policy year. The result is then multiplied by the interest index factor to determine the interest rate to be credited to the policy. Interest is credited at the end of the policy year and compounds annually.

However, you don't receive any of the dividend income from the stocks that make up the S&P 500 Index, so the return is actually somewhat less than the return on the S&P 500.

Jefferson Pilot guarantees that:

- The minimum surrender value at the end of the first eight-year term will be at least 114 percent of the premium (assuming you haven't made any withdrawals).

- If the S&P 500 declines, the accumulation value at the end of each term won't be lost.

- Equity indexed earnings will never be less than 0 percent during any given year.

- Equity indexed interest is linked to the average of the monthly S&P 500 values.
- The interest index factor will last through the entire eight-year term.

There are also several liquidity features available in some states, provided certain conditions are met. These include a 10 percent withdrawal provision each year, a nursing home/hospitalization confinement waiver, and a terminal illness waiver. There are also stiff penalties for early withdrawal, so you'll want to make sure that you only invest money you can afford to lock up for eight years. Because the interest is calculated annually, you won't receive any interest for the year on any money withdrawn before the end of the year.

For further information, contact a Jefferson Pilot Life representative or Wealth Transfer Planning, Inc., 11238 El Camino Real, Suite 200, San Diego, CA 92130; 619-350-4000 or 1-800-423-4890.

$CROOGE INVESTING TIP #146

Sell Your Investment, Pay No Capital Gains, and Get a Tax Deduction to Boot!

Here's a great tax shelter that avoids the capital gains tax completely while giving you a tax deduction and a secure income for life.

This technique is especially beneficial to retirees or people about to retire. You may have growth stocks or real estate that you want to sell. They may not pay much in income, and now that you are retired, you need more income. What to do?

Instead of selling your property or stocks and investing in bonds, try this alternative. Establish a special tax-exempt trust called a *charitable remainder trust* (CRT). Using a CRT, you donate your property to your favorite alma mater, foundation, church, or charity and obtain a lifetime income from it. A new type of CRT is available that is far more flexible than the old ones. I'm referring to a new CRT in which you can be your own trustee, make contributions at any time, and even change your beneficiaries during your lifetime.

Let's see the benefits of this program. Suppose you own growth stocks that you bought 15 years ago for $20,000, and they have a current market value of $200,000. Like most growth stocks, they pay only a small dividend, say 1 percent, so your growth stocks are currently paying you only $2000 a year. Because you want more income, you would like to sell your growth stocks and buy high-yielding bonds, which at 8 percent would pay you $16,000 a year.

But there's a problem. If you switch from stocks to bonds, you'll pay 20 percent in capital gains to Uncle Sam, plus more if your state has a capital-gains tax.

Because your cost basis (the original price you paid) is $20,000, you have a long-term gain of $180,000. You could owe the IRS a whopping $36,000, thousands of dollars lost forever. If you invest the remaining funds in an account paying 8 percent, you would earn $13,120 a year, substantially more than $2000 but much less than the $16,000 you would get annually if you didn't have to pay the capital gains tax at all.

Now let's see how valuable this new CRT can be. You transfer the growth stocks to your CRT, and the trustee (you or your appointed trustee) sells them through a broker. By using this trust vehicle, you completely avoided the capital gains tax. In addition, you receive an immediate tax deduction for setting up this charitable trust, based on the amount you donate. The deduction is determined by IRS tables and depends on your age and the amount of the investment.

The trustee of the CRT then purchases an income fund and pays you 8 percent a year in income, in this case, the full $16,000 a year for the rest of your life.

If you have additional stocks, real estate, or other assets you wish to sell, you can donate them to the same trust and boost your income further.

When you die, the assets in the CRT go to your favorite charity, whether it is your alma mater, a church, a hospital, or a public foundation. In this special CRT, you can name one or several charitable organizations as beneficiaries. As an added bonus, the assets going to charity are not subject to federal estate taxes.

You can start your own CRT with as little as $5000 and add to it as often as you like. Each time you do, you'll get an annual tax deduction, avoid capital gains taxes, and obtain more spendable income. The cost is a one-time setup fee of $300, plus an annual administrative fee based on the market value of the trust's assets (ranging from 0.012 to 0.8 percent).

For more information, contact David T. Phillips & Co., 3200 N. Dobson Rd., Building C, Chandler, AZ 95224; 800-223-9610.

$CROOGE INVESTING TIP #147

Get a Big Tax Write-Off on Appreciated Art
Under the 1993 tax act (which raised taxes in most cases), you can take a full deduction on the fair market value of art and collectibles donated to charity. Museums, art galleries, libraries, and churches can take full advantage of this new change.

Here's how it works. Let's suppose you bought an artwork for $10,000 several years ago. Now, you obtain an appraisal at fair market value of $35,000. If you are in the 45 percent tax bracket (state and federal), you would receive a reduction in taxes of $15,750 if you donate the piece to charity. Hence, by spending $10,000, you can cut your tax bill by $15,750. By donating your artwork, you put $5750 in your pocket.

For this tax break to qualify, the IRS requires the following:

1. You must hold your artwork for at least a year before donating.

2. You must donate your art to an IRS-approved charity (most foreign charities don't qualify).

3. The museum, library, or art gallery must state that it
    plans to display the artwork rather than sell it. If the
    charitable organization sells the artwork, the deduction
    may be disallowed.

Fine Arts Ltd. (recommended in Chapter 11) will assist
you with every stage of the donation process, from acquisi-
tion to placement with a charity of your choice. They have
been doing it successfully for years. Contact Michael B.
Kuschmann, President, Fine Arts Ltd., 174 West Comstock
Ave., Winter Park, FL 32789; 800-229-4322.

$CROOGE INVESTING TIP #148

**How to Find the Lowest-Cost Tax Preparation and Representative
(in Case You're Audited)**

The cheapest way to do your taxes is to do them yourself.
Several excellent low-cost tax manuals are available to help
you. The best ones are the annuals put together by J. K.
Lasser & Co., H&R Block, and the Arthur Young accounting
firm, available at the beginning of the year in book form or
software in most major bookstores or computer stores. The
software packages are geared to run the numbers automatically for you!

These are sufficient for most people, particularly if your
income is mostly salary and your deductions are easy to
compute.

A more expensive resource is the storefront tax preparer,
such as the H&R Block chain. Preparation fees should not
exceed $100 in most cases. Don't expect any tax-planning
advice. Most of the people working in these offices are tem-
porary employees hired at tax time. H&R Block and similar
firms also offer full-time preparers, but you can expect to
pay at least $100 for their services.

The third option is an enrolled agent. Enrolled agents
must either have five years of continuous employment with
the IRS applying and interpreting the tax code, or they must

pass a two-day exam on taxes for individuals, small businesses, partnerships, and corporations. They also must take
30 hours of continuous education every year.

If you're self-employed, you may benefit from having an
enrolled agent. It's best to get referrals from friends and rel-
atives. You can also get a referral in your area from the
National Association of Enrolled Agents, 200 Orchard Ridge
Dr., Suite 302, Gaithersburg, MD 20878; 800-424-4339 or
301-212-9608; www.naea.org.

The fourth option is a certified public accountant (CPA).
They generally cost 25 percent more than enrolled agents,
but they're often worth it. CPAs are usually best for people
who want to be more aggressive in their tax planning.
Enrolled agents, most of whom have worked for the IRS,
generally are more conservative. Again, personal referrals
are the best way to find them, or check with the National
Society of Accountants, 1010 North Fairfax St., Alexandria,
VA 22314; 703-548-6400; www.nsacct.org.

Stay away from any tax preparer who guarantees a refund
or whose fee is a percentage of the refund.

The highest priced option is a tax attorney. Their fees can
run up to hundreds of dollars per hour. Generally, I don't recommend tax attorneys to prepare returns. Use your CPA or
enrolled agent for that. Attorneys lose their client privilege if
they do your tax return. You should hire a tax attorney to rep-
resent you before the IRS, especially if your return is complicated or involves large sums of money. I've found that tax
attorneys are worth their weight in gold in tax disputes with
the IRS. They are far more intimidating than CPAs!

$CROOGE INVESTING TIP #149

Use This Low-Cost Tax-Cutting Ploy for Precious Metals and Rare Coins
Did you buy precious metals or rare coins years ago at high
prices? Would you like to hang onto them and still take a tax
deduction for your losses? Here's what you can do.

Precious metals and rare coins do not fall under the wash-sales rule for securities. That means you can sell your metals or coins, buy them back, and still have a legitimate tax loss locked in for the rest of the year. Ordinarily, commissions for this type of trade are prohibitive, but there's one dealer who will do it for a nominal fee.

Asset Strategies International will handle the transaction for 2 percent for metals and 4 percent or more for rare coins, plus shipping. Normally, you would pay at least double that amount. For information, contact Asset Strategies International, 1700 Rockville Pike, Suite 400, Rockville, MD 20852; 800-831-0007 or 301-881-8600; www.assetstrategies.com.

CHAPTER

17

MORE DISCOUNTS AND BENEFITS FOR SCROOGE INVESTORS

Human felicity is produced not so much by great pieces of good fortune that seldom happen as by little advantages that occur every day.

—Ben Franklin

THE LIST OF WAYS you can cut investment costs and obtain free or near-free products and services is limited only by the imagination. The wise miser can find countless techniques. Here are a few more. Be resourceful.

$CROOGE INVESTING TIP #150

Join a Club for Discounts

A few organizations offer you dozens of ways to reduce your investment costs. Here are some clubs that offer substantial benefits to investors:

• **American Association of Individual Investors (AAII)** (625 North Michigan Ave., Chicago, IL 60611;

312-280-0170; www.aaii.com). AAII has dozens of chapters throughout the country. I've spoken at many of its meetings, and it is always a great group of intelligent investors. This nonprofit organization offers several benefits to members, including a free monthly journal, a quote line that gives real-time price quotes for stocks, options, and mutual funds, several free books, reduced-cost investment seminars, and discounts on other services, such as its study programs and computer-users newsletter. Dues are only $49 a year; $490 for a lifetime membership.

- **National Association of Investors Corporation (NAIC)** (P.O. Box 220, Royal Oak, MI 48068; 877-275-6242; www.better-investing.org). If you want to start your own investment club, this is the organization to join. Since 1951, NAIC has helped small investors form clubs to study the stock market and invest in common stocks. It offers a variety of publications and services at modest prices, including its magazine, *Better Investing.* NAIC also offers discounts on group insurance plans and study-travel tips. Write for a brochure or check the Web site.

- **American Association of Retired Persons (AARP)** (601 E St. NW, Washington, DC 20049; 800-424-3410 or 202-434-2277; www.aarp.org). This is not an organization I can endorse because AARP frequently supports legislation favoring retired people at the expense of the rest of the nation. However, it does offer several advantages to investors. AARP offers a variety of cut-rate services due to its nonprofit status, including IRAs with no custodial fees. A large-print prospectus is available. AARP also offers a VISA card from BancOne with no annual fee and a 13.99 percent annual interest rate, plus a long-term commitment to keep that rate low (call 800-283-2318 for details). Health, auto, homeowner, and medical insurance are also available, as well as travel discounts and drugstore bargains. Membership is only $8 a year and is open to anyone over 50.

An alternative seniors' organization is **United Seniors Association (USA)** (3900 Jermantown Rd., Suite 450, Fairfax, VA 22033; 703-359-6500; www.unitedseniors.com). It has over 650,000 members, and the annual membership fee is only $5. They don't offer as many services as AARP, but they do offer discounts on travel, hotels, car rentals, prescription drugs, etc.

- **United States Automobile Association (USAA)** (9800 Fredericksburg, San Antonio, TX 78288; 800-531-8080). Founded in 1922, USAA is a huge member-owned cooperative offering low rates on insurance, mutual funds, and other financial services. *Forbes* magazine once described it as "a financial supermarket—a one-stop shop for everything from stocks to life insurance."

  Membership is open to active or former military officers and their dependents, but you don't have to be a member to take advantage of most of the investment services. Some life and health insurance, pure no-load mutual funds, banking services, real estate products, and the discount brokerage service are available to non-members. However, only members and associate members are eligible for the casualty, property, and auto insurance products and for the buying club.

$CROOGE INVESTING TIP #151

Use Fee-Only Financial Planners

If you need help putting together a financial plan, it's best to go to a fee-only planner. You're likely to pay far less in the long run for a planner who charges a flat or hourly fee than you will for one who makes a living by selling high-commission products. As always, it's a good idea to shop around. Talk to at least three financial planners.

Fee-only planners are sometimes hard to find. Expect to pay from $100 to $175 an hour and a minimum of $2500 total for a comprehensive plan. You should always get references and check them out before putting down any money. Of course, you can get lower-cost plans, including some computerized plans, but these usually leave you to do most of the work.

You can find a fee-only planner through the National Association of Personal Financial Advisors (NAPFA) (355 West Dundee Rd., Suite 200, Buffalo Grove, IL 60089; 800-366-2732 or 708-537-7722; www.napfa.org). Call or write for a referral in your area. Also ask for your free copy of a list of the tough questions to ask prospective planners.

There's just one problem with fee-only planners. Some of them go beyond recommending investments and actually help structure investment deals. They may not be earning a commission, but they still stand to gain by charging management and other fees. If any planner recommends a limited partnership, make sure that he doesn't have any interest in it.

$CROOGE INVESTING TIP #152

Own One Share of These Companies and Receive Incredible Benefits
Not all companies are created equal. Some publicly traded companies offer great fringe benefits and discounts to their shareholders.

- Marriott takes $10 off weekend stays at Marriott Hotels if you are a shareholder, a 10 percent discount at Fairfield Inns, and a 10 percent discount on weekend stays at Courtyard hotels.

- Wrigley sends all shareholders a free box of 20 packs of chewing gum each year.

- Disney shareholders can obtain a Magic Kingdom Club Gold Card for $39 a year, entitling holders to a variety of discounts and free services at Disney resorts.

- Ralston Purina, the dog food company, offers 30 percent off accommodations at its ski resort, the Keystone Resort in Colorado.

- CSX offers special "house parties" for its shareholders at certain times during the year at its famous resort, The Greenbriar, in West Virginia. Special discount rates apply.

- Brown-Forman provides a 50 percent discount on its Hartmann luggage.

- Tandy offers shareholders a 10 percent holiday discount on purchases up to $10,000 at its Radio Shack stores in December.

- Colgate-Palmolive, Gerber Products, 3M, Kellogg, Quaker Oaks, General Mills, Kimberly-Clark, and Scott Paper are among the companies that send out discount coupons and goody bags at times.

Want more examples? See *Free Lunch on Wall Street: Perks, Freebies, and Giveaways for Investors,* by Charles B. Carlson (McGraw-Hill Order Services, 800-338-3987; $14.95, plus P&H and sales tax; or avoid the sales tax by ordering from www.amazon.com).

$CROOGE INVESTING TIP #153

How to Get a Computer for "FREE" (or at Least Dirt Cheap)!
Just as the Internet is changing the way we invest—for the better—it is also changing the way we shop for everything, including insurance, cars, airline tickets . . . you name it. If you're not connected to the Internet, you're missing out on the biggest consumer bonanza in history.

In fact, you can even get a FREE computer on the Internet. There are several Web sites you can go to and get a free computer. The catch is that (1) you must sign a long-term agreement for Internet access, and (2) you must provide certain information about yourself, which will then be used to target you for various products and services. In short, it works on the same principle as cellular phones: you get the phone for free, but you have to sign a long-term contract for cell-phone service.

The free computer gimmick is a tradeoff. The price that you'll pay for Internet service is about $10 higher than most of the leading Internet access providers, like America Online, charge. You'll also give up some of your privacy. And the free computer may not come with a monitor, and it certainly won't come with a printer. When all is said and done, you'll probably have spent about $1000 for your "free PC." That's not a bad price, but it's also not a super-bargain.

Apparently, though, the tradeoff is worth it for many people, because there are long waiting lists at many of the Web sites offering free PCs. Each offer is slightly different.

The computer you will get varies, but you can bet that it won't be state-of-the-art. It's an off-brand, middle-of-the-road computer that you can use for Internet access, word processing, and a few other applications. It won't be as fast or have as much memory as the higher-end computers.

One of the better offers is from a company called Free-PC (www.free-pc.com). The company gave away thousands of computers to people who said they would agree to having ads cover 30 percent of their monitor's screen at all times. Again, though, you must answer lots of personal questions and give up some of you privacy to get the free PC.

Some of the Web sites offering free PCs include:

Direct Web (www.directweb.com)

FlashNet Communications (www.flash.net)

Shopps.com (www.shopss.com)

InterSQUID.com (www.intersquid.com)

Gobi (www.gobi.com)

Microworkz (www.microworkz.com)

Micro Center (www.microcenter.com)

Circuit City (www.circuitcity.com)

CompUSA (www.compusa.com)

Lan Plus (www.epcdirect.com)

Of course, you could just buy an inexpensive PC and avoid the hassle. For example, the Compaq Presario 5000 series is available for about $600, including a modem. Add on $200 for a monitor and $100 for a printer and you've got a complete setup for under $1000. The Apple iMac, which comes with a modem and monitor, costs about $1200. A good source for mail order computers are the catalogs from PC Connection and Mac Connection (1-800-800-0009).

$CROOGE INVESTING TIP #154

Get FREE Internet Access
Free Internet access is easier and a little more straightforward than getting a free computer. Typically, Internet access costs about $20 a month. Some Internet service providers (ISPs) give you unlimited Internet access. Others give you only a certain number of hours free and then charge you extra if you go over that amount. If you plan to surf the Web a lot, go with an ISP that offers unlimited net access.

Some ISPs you might want to consider include America Online (1-800-827-6364), Earthlink (1-800-395-8425), or Mindspring (1-888-677-7464). When you call them, ask about their free trial.

You can also get full, unlimited Internet access for free, if you don't mind having an advertising banner appear on your computer every time you're online. It's available from NetZero. Just go to its Web site (www.netzero.com) and follow the instructions to download your free software. You will need a computer with an Internet browser installed, either Netscape Navigator or Internet Explorer. And make sure you read the fine print. For example, if you try to get rid of the ad window, you'll be in for a nasty surprise: a fee of $59.95 per month for as long as you keep the service.

$CROOGE INVESTING TIP #155

Get FREE E-mail, Voicemail, and Faxes

Once you're online, you can get other free services.

A free e-mail address is offered by hundreds of sites on the Internet. Two of the most popular include Hotmail (www.hotmail.com) and Yahoo!Mail (www.yahoo.com).

Less known are the free fax and free (or low-cost) voice-mail available on the Internet.

You can send faxes over the Internet for free, using eFax (www.efax.com).

Several companies offer free voicemail, but you will need a sound card and speakers on your computer to use it. RocketTalk, which is based in Fullerton, California, is one of these companies. For details, go to its Web site at www. rockettalk.com.

If you're a traveler, you might check out the free voicemail and e-mail offered by Lonely Planet, the travel guidebook publisher based in Melbourne, Australia. You can access your voicemail or e-mail account free over the Internet and through toll-free telephone numbers in 60 countries. Go to www. lonelyplanet.com.

$CROOGE INVESTING TIP #156

Make the Most of Frequent Flyer Programs

Frequent flyer miles are a godsend to cheapskates. What's more, mileage is getting easier to earn and easier to cash in. Two major airlines, TWA and American, give their loyal customers miles that never expire. That's like money in the bank.

In fact, these days, you don't even need to leave the ground to earn thousands of airline miles. You can earn miles when you buy a computer, order a mattress, buy home furnishings, order flowers, make long-distance telephone calls, or even buy a Brink's security system for your home. In fact, frequent flyer miles are now attached to over 5000 products and services.

Consider the following:

- At many airlines, you can eat your way to free flights. Several airlines have partnered with select restaurants, offering free mileage (three miles for every dollar spent) to diners at these establishments. You can charge these meals on your airline credit card, of course, and earn more miles. Randy Peterson, publisher of the magazine *Inside Flyer,* says that you can earn 25,000 miles—enough for a free airline ticket—by spending just $50 a week dining out. If you dine out that much anyway, why not get a free airline ticket for it. Check out the magazine's Web site (www.webflyer.com) for details on this and other ways to get the most of your frequent flyer miles.

- Many airlines have partnered with discount brokers to offer frequent flyer miles to investors. Typically, you can earn one mile for every $10 worth of stock you buy. American, Delta, and TWA all have such programs with select discount brokers.

- You can get frequent flyer miles when you buy or sell your house or take out a mortgage. American Airlines is offering one mile for every dollar of interest paid on mortgages obtained through participating lenders. Or you can earn 15,000 miles for every $100,000 of a home purchase price through a participating broker.

$CROOGE INVESTING TIP #157

Join the Frequent Flyer Mileage Program at All the Major Airlines
It costs you nothing to open a frequent flyer mileage account at any airline. So you might as well do it. The IRS hasn't figured out a way to tax you for frequent flyer miles, so earning them is like earning tax-free money.

Here are the major airlines, along with their toll-free numbers and Web sites:

Alaska Airlines (www.alaskaair.com); 1-800-654-5669

American Airlines (www.aa.com); 1-800-882-8880

America West (www.americawest.com); 1-800-247-5691

Continental Airlines (www.onepass.com); 1-800-525-0280

Delta Airlines (www.delta-air.com); 1-800-325-3999

Northwest Airlines (www.nwa.com); 1-800-447-3757

Trans World Airlines (www.twa.com); 1-800-325-4815

United Airlines (www.ual.com); 1-800-421-4655

US Airways (www.usairways.com); 1-800-872-4738

While it's good to join these programs just to see what each one offers and compare them, unless you fly a lot, you're probably better off if you don't spread yourself too thin and try to accumulate miles on more than a couple of them.

When you've decided on a couple of programs, learn all you can about them and sign up for affiliated credit cards that earn you miles (see tip #159).

Once you've accumulated enough miles and you're ready to cash in, you'll be most successful if you are flexible, especially on popular routes or during heavy travel periods. Try to plan your travel well in advance or else travel during the off-season. Be willing to change planes and endure long layovers. Look for special deals. If an airline is flying a new route or offering large discounts on fares, you'll find it easier to get free miles. Check your favorite airlines' Web sites frequently for new information, rather than just waiting for their newsletters.

$CROOGE INVESTMENT TIP #158

Capitalize on More Ways to Save Money on Airfares and Other Travel Expenses

The Internet is a great resource for bargain travelers, especially if you can cut through the clutter. Some airlines are offering ultrabargain fares on their Web sites that aren't available anywhere else. By booking your own travel online, you can often cut out the middleman, the travel agent. Some airlines are even offering additional mileage for flights booked online.

While the Internet isn't always as easy or as comprehensive as getting on the phone and doing your own research, it's a good place to start. For example, you can go to a Web site like bestfares.com (www.bestfares.com); type in where you want to go, your departure date, and your arrival date; and you'll get back the best airfare.

Not all travel Web sites offer negotiated fares, sales fares, consolidater fares, and vacation packages that link low fares with lodging. One that does is 1travel.com (www.1travel. com), with its Farebeater search engine and its Airline Savings Toolkit. It will also help you find alternative airports.

Many of the following Web sites help you book not only airfares but also lodging and rental cars for big savings:

Biztravel.com (www.biztravel.com)

Cheaptickets Online (www.cheaptickets.com)

Expedia Travel (www.expedia.com)

Internet Travel Network (www.itn.com)

Preview Travel (www.previewtravel.com)

Priceline.com (www.priceline.com)

Travelocity.com (www.travelocity.com)

$CROOGE INVESTING TIP #159

Use the Best Air-Miles Cards

One type of rebate card is the air-miles card, which pays you in frequent flyer miles instead of cash. If you travel a lot, that's as good as getting cash. There are several cards that offer air miles for traveling on all the major airlines. Some of the better ones include:

Chase (1-800-438-3535), which charges the prime rate plus 7.49 percent (currently 19.3 percent). It charges a $25 annual fee and awards a domestic round-trip ticket after you've earned 25,000 points.

Travel Choices VISA (1-800-349-2632), which charges the prime rate plus 8.99 percent (currently 19.8 percent), a $25 annual fee, and awards domestic round-trip tickets for 25,000 points.

USAA Eagle Points (1-800-793-8990), which charges the prime rate plus 5.55 percent (currently 13.25 percent), charges a $49 annual fee, and gives you a ticket after you've racked up 25,000 points.

$CROOGE INVESTING TIP #160

With Life Insurance, Determine If It Is Advantageous or Not to Buy Term and Invest the Difference

The standard advice for years has been to buy term insurance and invest the difference in stocks or mutual funds. It is still excellent advice for many people. However, cash-value life insurance, on which money accrues over the life of the policy, offers some distinct advantages.

1. If you have trouble saving money, it forces you to save.

2. Taxes are deferred on the increase in the cash value of your life insurance.

3. The money that you invest is earning money for both you and the insurance company.

4. You can borrow against the cash value of your policy, although the interest charged will be greater than the interest your money earned.

Wealthy families (estates of over $650,000 in 1999, gradually increasing to $1 million in 2006) can use life insurance to avoid estate taxes and pay probate expenses (state inheritance tax laws vary, so consult your attorney if you're interested in the details).

Thus, you should not ignore cash-value life insurance. Although the advice to buy term and invest the difference still works for many people, especially people between their twenties and forties, it may not necessarily be the best for you.

$CROOGE INVESTING TIP #161

How to Get the Best Deal on Term Insurance

As this book is being prepared, a rate war is raging in term insurance. Of course, that's good news for consumers. Rates are at all-time lows. It's a buyer's market!

It's easy to compare policies for term insurance. Several companies will give you quotes from different insurers. All you do is call them and answer a few questions, such as your age, whether or not you smoke, and the amount of coverage you need. Within a week, you'll receive a printout containing information on several of the least expensive, highly rated insurance companies. Here is your contact information.

- **Insurance Quote Services** (3200 N. Dobson Rd., Bldg. C, Chandler, AZ 85224; 800-972-1104, 602-345-7241; www.iquote.com) has been in business for 25 years and is run by David T. Phillips & Company, a pioneer in low-cost insurance shopping. It will send you, by mail, fax, or e-mail, a list of the five cheapest term policies from companies rated A+ by A. M. Best.

- **Select Quote Insurance Services** (595 Market Street, 5th Floor, San Francisco, CA 94105; 800-343-1985, 415-543-7338; www.selectquote.com) will send five quotes for each of two policy face amounts.

- **INSurance INFOrmation** (Cobblestone Court #2, 23 Route 134, South Dennis, MA 02660; 800-472-5800, 508-394-9117; www.insuranceinformation.com). Of the three, this is the only one that charges for quotes. The fee is $50, refundable if it can't find a policy cheaper than your current one. This is strictly a referral service; it is the only one of the three that doesn't sell insurance.

Bear in mind that the cheapest first-year term policy is not necessarily the cheapest over a five- or ten-year period. Check the rates for each year.

18

CONCLUSION: THE PHILOSOPHY OF THE SCROOGE INVESTOR IN THE NEW MILLENNIUM

Work for yourself. Satisfy your customers. Be thrifty in all things.
Leave the world a better place than you found it.

—*J. Paul Getty*

IN THE PREVIOUS 17 CHAPTERS, we have applied the Scrooge philosophy to a wide variety of invest-ments—stocks, bonds, mutual funds, real estate, pre-cious metals, and foreign investments. In a very real sense, the Scrooge philosophy should encompass all your financial activities.

What is this Scrooge philosophy?

- Scrooge Investors are productive citizens, always seek-ing opportunities to make money by offering goods or services that people can really use.

- Scrooge Investors look for new trends and opportunities ahead of the crowd (like computers, the Internet, and biotechnology).

- Scrooge Investors keep track of their expenses, down to the last penny.

- Scrooge Investors always live within their means, avoiding wasteful expenditures.

- Scrooge Investors avoid consumer debt like the plague, paying in cash whenever possible.

- Scrooge Investors borrow money for business purposes only when absolutely essential and then make sure their earnings always exceed their interest expenses.

- Scrooge Investors are always cost-conscious in business, investments, and their personal affairs. Scrooge Investors increase their net worth each month, no matter how much they spend.

- Scrooge Investors develop a consistent savings program.

- Scrooge Investors take advantage of the knowledge and wisdom of the best experts in their fields.

- Scrooge Investors stay in good physical and mental shape, knowing that if you're not healthy, you're not wealthy.

- Scrooge Investors are suspicious of government agents and their urge to tax, spend, regulate, and control our lives.

- Last but not least, Scrooge Investors are computer literate. That's the biggest lesson to learn from this third edition of *Scrooge Investing*.

FAMOUS SCROOGE INVESTORS

You can find many examples of wealthy individuals who have followed this advice. I've referred already to fictional characters who have followed the Scrooge philosophy. What about real-life examples?

John D. Rockefeller, Jr., the oil magnate who became America's first billionaire, was always cost-conscious. He always had big goals. To achieve them, he worked hard and looked for exciting new opportunities. Discipline, order, and thrift were habits he formed early in life. He kept a financial journal, Ledger A, in which he wrote down, day-by-day and to the penny, his income, expenses, savings, investments, and business affairs. He was careful not to spend too much on clothing and other consumer goods. In short, he was destined for financial independence.

J. Paul Getty, another oil billionaire, had extensive experience in all areas of business and investing. He was a high-flying speculator but always practiced economy and discipline and used others' expertise. "Make your money first; then think about spending it," he advised. He was a hard worker: "I still find it's often necessary to work 16 to 18 hours a day, and sometimes around the clock." Getty was an inveterate bargain hunter. In the stock market, he bought stocks during the 1930s depression when everyone else was scared. "Get-rich-quick schemes just don't work," he said. He recommended buying low-priced stocks in "industries that cannot help but burgeon as time goes on."

John Templeton, who runs one of the most successful mutual funds in history, is a strong believer in the Scrooge philosophy. During the 1930s depression, he saved 50 percent of his income! He avoids consumer debt. In fact, he bought his first home with cash. He works hard, putting in 60 hours a week. In selecting stocks, he looks for companies around the world that offer low prices and an excellent long-term outlook. "If you're going to buy the best bargains, look in more than one industry, and look in more than one nation." He adds, "Avoid investing in those countries with a high level of socialism or government regulation of business."

Warren Buffett, the Omaha billionaire, takes a strong business approach to investing. He also works long hours. He learned frugality from his father, a congressman who strongly opposed government waste. Buffett concentrates on only a few companies and gets to know them well. He avoids poorly managed companies, no matter how enticing the bargain price. "We try to buy not only good businesses, but ones run by high-grade, talented, and likeable managers." According to Buffett, good managers are dedicated cost-cutters who know the budget of everything in their company. Just as cost-conscious businesses are the most profitable, cost-conscious investors are the most successful. He searches for stocks that can be bought for less than they're worth. When buying a company, Buffett takes a conservative approach. Instead of buying common stocks, for example, he often buys preferred convertible stock, which earns income, limits his downside risk, and offers upside potential.

STINGY OR JUST CAREFUL?

The greatest temptation facing every Scrooge Investor is to be too much of a skinflint, unwilling to let go of any money. Before his repentance and change of heart, Ebenezer Scrooge adamantly refused to give anything to charity. "Bah, humbug!" he responded. "I wish to be left alone." It is clear that Charles Dickens's famous character was not a happy man.

Every Scrooge Investor must discover, as did the original Scrooge, that happiness is achieved by living life to the fullest. Most important, he must learn to enjoy leisure time. As the Chinese philosopher Lin Yutang says in *The Importance of Living:*

> O wise humanity, terribly wise humanity! Of thee I sing. How inscrutable is the civilization where men toil and work and worry their hair gray to get a living and forget to play!

This change in attitude also means an appreciation for the free enterprise system, which gives one the chance to be financially successful. Without freedom, a sound legal system, and a stable political environment, very few prosper. Most business people and investors suffer. Just as the shrewd gambler always leaves something on the table, the wise investor should return some money to the system through charitable giving or donations to foundations dedicated to free enterprise.

Arkad, the main character in *The Richest Man in Babylon,* expresses the true spirit of financial stewardship when he states, "A part of all you earn is yours to keep." Note that he said "a part," not all. George Clason, the author of this classic, the greatest financial book ever written, describes Arkad's approach as follows: "In old Babylon there once lived a certain very rich man named Arkad. Far and wide he was famed for his great wealth. Also, was he famed for his liberality. He was generous with his family. He was liberal in his own expenses. But nevertheless each year his wealth increased more rapidly than he spent it."

It is possible and even prudent to follow Arkad's lead. You can be generous in your expenditures and still become richer every year. It's not how much you earn or even how much you spend that really matters. It's how much you keep. If you are going to keep anything, you must follow the Scrooge philosophy in everything you do: *Always spend less than you earn!*

Index

AccuTrade, 57
AIM funds, 54
Alliance group, 54
America Online, 11
American Association of Individual
　Investors (AAII), 56, 209–210
American Association of Retired Persons
　(AARP), 198, 210–211
American Depositary Receipts (ADRs), 43
Ameritrade, 37–39, 42, 57, 197
Annuities, 199–202
Art and collectibles, 151–163
　charitable donations of, 204–206
　limited editions, 156–157, 162–163
Asian crisis (1997), 10, 23
Asset Strategies International, 207
Atlanta Investment Conference, 115–116
AT&T Universal platinum card, 188
Auctions, 157–162
Auto loans, 80

Back-end loads, 46–47
Bahamas bank accounts, 176
Band, Richard, 21
Banking services, 80–85
　checking, 82–85, 176–177
　foreign bank accounts, 165, 169–171,
　　174–176
　foreign currency investment, 166–169
　foreign safe deposit boxes, 165, 171–174
　mortgages, 80, 81, 144–146
　offshore VISA debit cards, 176–177
Bankruptcy, 5, 8, 19, 32, 76–77
Barks, Carl, 1–4
Barron's, 21, 24, 25, 94, 95, 102, 163
Barry Murphy & Company, Inc., 37–39, 42,
　43, 197
Bear markets, 8, 9, 12
Big Charts, 108
Blackrock Insured Muni Bond Fund, 67

Blanchard, Jim, 117
Bloomberg, 106, 110
Blumert, Bert, 132
Bonds, 63–77
　government policy and, 9
　mutual funds, 65–70, 195
Borrowing, 183–191
　credit cards and, 80, 81, 161, 167, 169,
　　187–191
　from margin accounts, 122, 185
　mortgages and, 80, 81, 144–146,
　　148–149, 185–186, 217
Bradford, R. W., 163
Brady Bonds, 77
Brown & Company, 37–39, 41, 42, 92
Buffett, Warren, 4–5, 19, 196, 225–226
Bush Burns, 57
Business Week, 30
Buying Right (Schaub), 143

Capital gains taxes, 194, 202–205
Carlson, Charles B., 213
Cash and cash equivalents, 79–88
　coins, 129–139, 206–207
　credit cards, 80, 81, 161, 167, 169,
　　187–191
　foreign bank accounts, 165, 169–171,
　　174–176
　foreign currencies, 166–169, 176–177
　offshore VISA debit cards, 176–177
　traveler's checks, 167, 168
CBS MarketWatch, 106
Certified Fraud Examiners, 111
Channel Islands bank accounts, 175–176
Charitable donations, 202–206
Charles Schwab & Co., 35–36, 37–39, 40,
　41, 42, 46, 51, 58, 60–61, 92
Christie's Fine Art Auctioneers, 158, 159,
　161, 162
Christmas Carol, A (Dickens), 2

Chrysler, 76
Churning, 121–122
Clason, George, 227
Closed-end funds, 10–11
  country funds, 23–24, 54
  discounts on, 21–25
  dividend reinvestment plans (DRIPs) for,
    25–27
  in high-load fund families, 53–54
  income funds, 24
  municipal bond, 65, 67, 72
  new issues of, 24–25
  (*See also* Mutual funds)
Clubs, 56, 198, 209–211
Coins:
  commemorative and proof, 163
  foreign safe deposit boxes for, 171–174
  precious metals, 129–139
  rare, 153–154, 163
  tax-cutting tips, 133, 134–136, 206–207
Collectibles (*see* Art and collectibles)
Commissions:
  auction, 159
  on commodity funds, 124
  of discount brokers, 35–36, 37–39, 40,
    92
  on dividend reinvestment plans, 25–27
  on futures, 127
  on new issues, 19, 20, 24–25
  in online trading, 92
  on options, 121–122, 127
Commodity bonds, 64–65
Commodity futures, 8, 121–127
  discount brokers, 125–126, 133–136,
    137
  information on trading, 122–123,
    133–136, 137
Compaq Computers, 8–9
Computers:
  free or cheap, 213–215
  (*See also* Internet access)
Conservative investors, 7–10
Contingent deferred sales charges, 46–47
Contrarian approach, 11–12
Contrarian Investment Strategies (Dreman),
  17–18
Convertible bonds, 72
Convertible Holdings Capital, 21–23
Convertible preferred stock, 66–67
Country funds, 23–24, 54
Coxon, Terry, 87
Credit cards, 80, 81, 187–191
  for auction purchases, 161
  extra charges, 169
  frequent flyer programs and, 217, 218
  purchasing foreign currency with, 167
Credit reports, 184–185

Currency markets:
  Asian, 10, 23
  coins as investments, 129–139, 206–207
  currency for travel, 167–169, 176–177
  European, 12–13
  foreign currency as investment, 166–169

Day trading, 93, 97–99
Developing-nation debt funds, 77
Dickens, Charles, 2, 226
Direct purchase plans (DPPs), 25–26
Discount brokers, 35–43
  as agent versus principal, 31
  art and collectible, 155–157
  borrowing from margin accounts, 185
  commissions of, 35–36, 37–39, 40, 92
  commodity, 125–126, 133–136, 137
  frequent flyer programs and, 217
  lists of, 42, 125
  mutual fund, 52–53, 55–58, 60–61
  new issues and, 19–20
  online services, 40, 92–99
  penny stocks and, 31
  stock option, 126–127
  survey of, 31, 37–39
  Touch-Tone trading with, 40, 97
Discount clubs, 56, 198, 209–211
Dividend reinvestment plans (DRIPs), 25–27
DLJ Direct, 37–39, 41, 42, 57
Dreman, David, 17–18
Dreyfus, 51, 56, 84–85
Dual-purpose funds, 21–23

E-mail, free, 216
eBay, 159, 160, 161
Emerging markets, 9–10, 68–69, 77
Escrow services, 160
E*Trade Securities, Inc., 37–39, 42, 104

Faxes, free, 216
Federal Trade Commission (FTC), 111
Fidelity, 35–36, 37–39, 41, 42, 51, 85
Financial planners, 211–212
Financial Times, The, 177–178
Fine Arts Ltd., 205
First Australia Prime Income Fund, 65–66
Firstar Bank, 166, 169
Fisher, Philip, 63
Fitch IBCA, 72
Floating rate funds, 68–69
Forbes, 17–18, 19, 30, 46, 47, 102
Forecasts and Strategies (newsletter), 22,
  65–67
Foreign income funds, 68–69
Foreign stocks, discount brokers and, 43
401(k) plans, 186–187, 197–198
Franklin, Benjamin, 5, 29, 79, 188, 209

Fraud prevention, 109–112, 159–161
Free Lunch on Wall Street (Carlson), 213
FreeEdgar, 108
Freeport McMoRan, 66–67
Frequent flyer programs, 216–220
Friedman, Milton, 91
Full-service brokerages, 35–36, 41, 75
Futures (*see* Commodity futures)

Gardner, David and Tom, 105
General Motors, 8
Getty, J. Paul, 4–5, 7, 18, 223, 225
Gold, 10, 66
    coins, 129–133, 136–139
    foreign safe deposit boxes for, 165,
        171–174
    government policy and, 9
    Web sites on, 138–139
Gomez Advisors Internet Broker Scorecard,
    94–95, 127
Government policy, 9–10, 77
Guaranteed stock index annuities, 201–202

Hall, David, 132
Handbook for No-Load Fund Investors, The
    (Jacobs), 47
High Income Advantage Trust, 65
Home Buyers Mortgage Kit, 144–145
How to Shop for Your Mortgage, 145
H&R Block, 205
Hyman, Tony, 154

IBM, 8
Importance of Living, The (Lin Yutang), 226
Income funds, 24
Index funds, 48–53, 105, 195
Initial public offerings (IPOs) (*see* New
    issues)
Insurance:
    for auction purchases, 160–161
    for bank accounts, 167
    for foreign safe deposit boxes, 171–172
    term life insurance, 220–222
    variable annuities, 200–201
    variable universal life (VUL), 199–200
Interactive Collector, 159, 162
Interest rates:
    on credit cards, 187, 189–190
    prime rate funds, 67–68
    Web sites on, 183–185, 186, 187
International Investment Conferences, 116
Internet access:
    crashproofing online brokerage accounts,
        91–92, 95–97, 126
    free, 215
    with "free" computers, 213–215
    free e-mail, voicemail, and faxes, 216

Internet Fraud Watch, 111, 159–161
Intershow, 116–117
Invest in Debt (Napier), 149
Investment information, 101–117
    on art and collectibles, 152–153
    false information, 109–111
    from investment seminars and
        conferences, 113–117
    libraries and, 102–103
    magazines, 108–109
    from message boards, 109–111, 112–113
    newsletters, 22, 31–32, 47, 65–67, 103,
        130, 143, 153–154, 178–179
    on penny stocks, 32–33
    on trading futures and options, 122–123,
        133–136, 137
    Web sites on, 103–108, 111–113
    (*See also specific types of investments*)
Investment Protection Trust, 111
Isle of Man bank accounts, 175–176

Jack White & Co., 58
Jacobs, Sheldon, 47
Jefferson-Pilot Life, 201–202
Jim Blanchard's New Orleans Investment
    Conference, 117
John Nuveen & Co. Incorporated, 70–71
Johnson, Samuel, 45
Junk bonds, 65, 74

Ketcher, Mike, 174
Keynes, John Maynard, 91
KnowX, 112
Kuschmann, Michael B., 155–157, 205

Lease options, 146–147, 185
Life insurance:
    term, 220–222
    variable universal life (VUL), 199–200
Limit orders, 40
Lin Yutang, 226
Lipper, Inc., 50
Liquidity, of penny stocks, 33
Lloyds Bank Worldwide Service, 169–170
Lloyds of London, 171–172
Loans (*see* Borrowing)

Magma Copper, 64–65
Managed accounts, 196
Managed commodity accounts, 124–125
Margin calls, 122, 185
Market capitalization:
    defined, 32–33
    large-cap, with low P/E ratio stocks,
        17–18
    of penny stocks, 32–33
Market Guide, 108

Market makers, 31
Market orders, 40, 73
Markup:
  on art and collectibles, 151–152
  on bonds, 64, 69, 73–74, 75, 76
  defined, 64
  on new issues, 20
  on penny stocks, 30–31
Merrill Lynch, 36, 41
Message boards, 109–111, 112–113
Microsoft Investor (MSN), 105
MidAmerica Commodity Exchange
    (MIDAM), 125–126
Mining stocks, 10, 33, 139
Money magazine, 30, 80, 94, 95, 102,
    108–109
Money market funds, 82–85
Moody's, 73, 74
Morningstar, 46, 59–60, 102, 106–107, 195
Mortgages:
  buying, 148–149
  frequent flyer programs and, 217
  as loans, 80, 81, 144–146, 148–149,
    185–186, 217
  second, 148–149
Motley Fool, 105, 113
Municipal bond funds, 65, 67, 72
Municipal bond trusts, 71
Muriel Siebert, 57
Mutual funds, 45–61
  annual expense ratios of, 46, 48, 49, 84
  bond, 65–70, 195
  commodity funds, 124–125
  index funds, 48–53, 105, 195
  investment information on, 102
  money market, 82–85
  real estate, 147
  short-term, 87–88
  taxes and, 48–50, 194–195
  (*See also* Closed-end funds)

Napier, Jim, 149
Nasdaq-Amex, 108
Nasdaq Index, 18
National Association of Securities Dealers
    (NASD), 73, 112
National Discount Brokers, 26–27, 37–39,
    41, 42, 57
National Futures Association, 112
Neill, Humphrey B., 12
Net asset value (NAV), 11
New issues:
  of bonds, 74
  of closed-end equity funds, 24–25
  commissions on, 19, 20, 24–25
  prospectuses, 74
  of stocks, 10–11, 19–21

Nissan Motors, 8–9
No-Load Fund Investor, The (newsletter),
    47

Offshore investments, 165–179
Olde Discount Stockbrokers, 37–39, 41, 42
Online brokers, 40, 91–99
  crashproofing accounts with, 91–92,
    95–97, 126
  futures, 126–127
  new issues and, 19–20
  options, 127
Online Investor magazine, 104–106, 109
Options, 8, 121–127
O'Shaughnessy, James P., 18
Over-the-counter (OTC) stocks, 18, 108
  American Depositary Receipts (ADRs), 43
  penny stocks, 10, 29–33

Palladium, 136–138, 165, 171–174
Pan Am, 8
Penny stocks, 10, 29–33
Perth Mint certificates, 172–174
Peterson, Randy, 217
Phillips, David T., 200, 204
Platinum, 136–139, 165, 171–174
Precious metals:
  coins, 129–139
  foreign safe deposit boxes for, 165,
    171–174
  futures on, 133–136, 137
  mining stocks, 10, 33, 139
  tax-cutting tip, 206–207
  (*See also specific metals*)
Preferred stock, convertible, 66–67
Price/earning (P/E) ratios, 17–18
Prime rate funds, 67–68
Prospectuses, 45, 46, 51, 53, 74, 104

Quantum Fund, 12–13
Quick & Reilly, 37–39, 42
Quicken, 105

Raging Bull, 113
Real estate, 141–149
  down payments on, 185–186
  government policy and, 9
  home equity loans, 186
  lease option, 146–147, 185
  mortgages, 80, 81, 144–146, 148–149,
    185–186, 217
Redemption fees, 46
Research (*see* Investment information)
Retirement planning:
  charitable remainder trusts (CRT),
    202–204
  fee-only financial planners and, 211–212

Retirement planning (*Cont.*):
  401(k) plans, 186–187, 197–198
  Roth IRAs, 194, 196–197, 198–199
  self-directed plans, 196–197
  seniors organizations, 198, 210–211
Richest Man in Babylon, The (Clason), 227
Rockefeller, John D., Jr., 4–5, 225
Roth IRAs, 194, 196–197, 198–199

Safe deposit boxes, foreign, 165, 171–174
Salomon Smith Barney, 41, 124
Savings accounts, 80
Schaub, John, 142–143, 146, 147, 149
ScotiaMocatta Delivery Orders, 171–173
Scottsdale Securities, Inc., 37–39, 41, 42
Scrooge philosophy of investing:
  famous Scrooge investors, 224–226
  origins of concept, 1–4
  penny-wise, pound-foolish approach
    versus, 5
  principles of, 4, 7, 223–224
Scudder, 52–53, 56, 200–201
Securities & Exchange Commission (SEC),
    107–108, 109, 112
Seneca, 35
Short selling, 8
Short-term funds, 87–88
Siegel, Jeremy, 49
Silicon Investor, 113
Silver, 66
  coins, 129–133, 136–139
  foreign safe deposit boxes for, 165, 171–174
  Web sites on, 138–139
Smart Money, 57, 94, 95, 107
Soros, George, 12–13
Sotheby's, 158, 159, 161, 162
Speculative investors, 8, 10, 12–13
Stock Detective, 112
Stock options, 8, 121–127
Stocks:
  closed-end funds, 10–11, 21–25
  dividend reinvestment plans (DRIPs) for,
    25–27
  foreign, 43
  government policy and, 9
  guaranteed stock index annuities and,
    201–202
  junior mining, 10, 33, 139
  large-cap, with low P/E ratios, 17–18
  margin accounts, 185
  mining, 10, 33, 139
  new issues, 10–11, 19–21
  over-the-counter, 10, 18, 29–33, 43, 108
  penny, 10, 29–33
  permanently undervalued, 8
  shareholder fringe benefits, 212–213
  short sales of, 8

Stocks (*Cont.*):
  tax considerations, 194–195, 196
Stockscape.com Technologies, 107
TheStreet, 107
Strong Funds, 51
Superdiscount brokers, 40–41
Swiss bank accounts, 165, 170–171

T. Rowe Price, 51
Taxes, 193–207
  on coins and bullion, 133, 134–136,
    206–207
  emerging markets and, 9–10
  government policy and, 9
  mutual funds and, 48–50, 194–195
  short-term funds and, 87–88
  zero-coupon bonds and, 75–76
Templeton, 54
Templeton, John, 225
Term life insurance, 220–222
TheStreet, 107
Touch-Tone trading, 40, 97
Travel:
  air-miles cards, 219–220
  currency conversion for, 167–169
  frequent flyer programs, 216–220
  offshore VISA debit cards, 176–177
  traveler's checks, 167, 168
Treasury bills, 85–87
Truax, Martin, 116, 124
12b-1 fees, 46

Uncle Scrooge McDuck: His Life and Times
    (Barks), 1–4
Unit investment trusts (UIT), 69–71
U.S. Global Investors, 51

Van Kampen Funds, Inc., 54, 65, 68, 70, 71
Vanguard, 37–39, 42, 51, 52–53, 56–57, 69,
    195, 197, 200
Variable annuities, 200–201
Variable universal life (VUL) insurance,
    199–200
Voicemail, free, 216

Wall Street City, 107
Wall Street Journal, The, 21, 24, 25, 30, 102
Wash-sales rule, 206–207
Waterhouse Securities, Inc., 31, 37–39,
    42–43, 57
Westhem, Andrew, 201
What Works on Wall Street (O'Shaughnessy),
    18

Yahoo!Finance, 106, 113
Young, Richard, 52

Zero-coupon bonds, 75–76

ABOUT THE AUTHOR

Mark Skousen has been a lifelong practitioner of the Scrooge philosophy. He has always believed in thrift, hard work, staying out of debt, and taking advantage of bargains. He started with very little and paid his way through college. When he graduated with honors, he had a fully paid-for new car, a full-time job, and money in his pocket—plus a fiancée who has been the secret to his success!

Today, Mark Skousen is financially independent and spends his time writing and researching investment and economic topics. He is the author of 20 books, including *High Finance on a Low Budget* (coauthored with his wife, Jo Ann), *The Complete Guide to Financial Privacy,* and *Economics on Trial.* He also is a contributor to *Forbes, The Wall Street Journal, Reason, Liberty,* and *Ideas on Liberty.*

Skousen received his Ph.D. in economics from George Washington University in 1977 and currently teaches economics and finance at Rollins College in Winter Park, Florida, where students often spot him driving around campus in his restored 1958 MGA automobile.

Professor Skousen also writes a monthly investment newsletter, *Forecasts & Strategies,* one of the largest financial letters in the country. In his spare time, he enjoys basketball, softball, collecting old books, and reading Uncle Scrooge comic books to his five children.

His personal Web site is www.mskousen.com, his newsletter Web site is www.forecasts-strategies.com, and his e-mail address is mskousen@mskousen.com.

126) XI, 127-2,3, 165 fee, 171 Book
176-8, 96